THE NIGHT BLOOMING

A Journey of Teen Twin Champions
Overcoming Racism, Rejection & Abuse,
To Find Their Identity & Purpose In Life

Sally and Jonah Ismael

THE NIGHT BLOOMING

A Journey of Teen Twin Champions
Overcoming Racism, Rejection & Abuse,
To Find Their Identity & Purpose In Life

by Sally and Jonah Ismael

Published by MultiEducator PRESS, New York

177A East Main Street • New Rochelle, NY 10801

Email: info@multied.com

© 2023 MultiEducator Press

ISBN # 978-1-885881-76-2

© 2023 All rights reserved by the authors Sally and Jonah Ismael

The right of Sally and Jonah Ismael to be identified as author of this work has been asserted (with exceptions in the case of the reading excerpts that are reprinted here with permission), in accordance with the US 1976 Copyright 2007 Act. No part of this book may be reproduced or utilized in any form or by any means, electronic or mechanical, or by any information storage and retrieval system without the prior permission of the publisher. The only exception to this prohibition is "fair use" as defined by U.S. copyright law.

TABLE OF CONTENTS

Foreward	6
Chapter One — Introduction	14
Chapter Two — Lost Identity	22
Chapter Three — The Beginning	28
Chapter Four — The Rejection	55
Chapter Five — The Isolation	77
Chapter Six — The Suffering	84
Chapter Seven — Our Story with Pain	105
Chapter Eight — The Process: Finding our Rhythm	131
Chapter Nine — Positivity is a Choice	140
Chapter Ten — Flowers Bloom at Night: Prosperity Comes from Healing	149
Chapter Eleven — Mentality is the Key: The Light at the End of the Tunnel	188
Chapter Twelve — The Power Within	205
Authors' Quotes	237

Acknowledgments

We dedicate every moment of hard work, determination, perseverance and passion to writing this book for our parents — those who believed in our dream. Thank you, our Father and our Mother, for your unconditional love, support, sacrifice, guidance, and encouragement.

To our wonderful teachers and Principal Mr. Matthew Conrad at Murphy Middle School, Principal of McMillen High School Mr. Todd Williams, and our Educators, Lorraine Searight, Veronica Godfrey, Peri Lobue, Maria Mata-Gonzalez, Kay Casey, Moi Liew, Ingrid Goslin, Tracie Redd, and Melissa Ait Belaid. We are so grateful, appreciative, and thankful for the endless positivity, love, support and encouragement you have given us.

Special thanks to our book editor Sara Kreisman, who worked tirelessly to edit the manuscript of our memoirs without changing anything in content or valuable events, and for her professionalism.

Our thanks go out to our publisher Marc Schulman for taking us step-by-step to bring this book to light, and for his efforts to guide us through the process.

Our most tremendous appreciation goes to Ms. Amy Erani. She was the icing on top of the cake. She gave her time, effort, and dedication to walk us step by step through the process of highlighting the important details of the book. Her creativity and passion for her work have added a positive environment to the process despite all the stress and pressure we were experiencing through the process of finalizing the book. Ms. Erani has a kind soul and a very calm spirit. Without her positivity, we couldn't have gone back through the painful memories in a very peaceful manner.

Our special words of acknowledgement go to our book's cover designer, Robin Sherman, who enveloped us with her love and support.

We are deeply grateful to the Congressional Awards Program, which motivated us to face our fears and doubts by inspiring us to continue writing and publishing our book. We set this goal of fulfilling our own personal development; however, we had a period of hesitation when we paused writing, as we were afraid to face rejection again. The Congressional Awards Program allowed us to find the strength to continue telling our story. This book could not have seen the light without pushing ourselves to work on our goals of personal development, despite how difficult they may have been.)

Words cannot express our gratitude to our Life Coach, our mother for her valuable advice, patience, emotional support and guidance. This book saw the light because of your constant inspiration and motivation. Thank you for sticking with us throughout these many years to embrace and advance our dream, and to constantly remind us of our purpose in life. Without your voice we could not survive and thrive. Thank you Mom for believing in us, in our story, in our talent, in our purpose in life, and encouraging us to use our voice through this book to reach out to many desperate children who need encouragement and motivation.

A Bit of History

For the past 2000 years, some form of martial arts always has been present in Korea. Today, this martial art form is known as Taekwondo. Taekwondo is a form of self-defense that uses flexible techniques performed with leg kicks. While Taekwondo is an ancient Korean martial art, in recent years it has developed into a modern international Olympic sport, known for its physical and mental discipline. Although Taekwondo is its own unique martial art form, it has been influenced by other forms such as Karate, Judo, and Kung Fu. Through physical and psychological exercise techniques, Taekwondo can strengthen values such as courtesy, loyalty, honesty, respect, trust, physical health, well-being, personal growth, and many more spiritual benefits — if taught the right way.

On April 11, 1955, modern Taekwondo was born. Since then, over 30 million people have practiced this sport in more than 156 countries. The ability to focus and concentrate are essential components of Taekwondo, but the physical essence of Taekwondo centers on kicking and punching. Kicking requires flexibility, speed, strength, and power. Through sparring, athletes need to demonstrate skillful kicking techniques in a very clever and situation-based manner. The journey to obtain a black belt takes years of practice and immense commitment, with athletes learning how to control every part of their bodies through the various forms they learn—forms developed through years of learning different types of kicks.

Foreword (Sally)

On a Friday evening in the summer of 2020, after we had finished our nightly training in our garage where we'd been training for over four years, Jonah (my twin brother and training partner) expressed his frustration with the sweltering heat. A very determined athlete, Jonah is always ready to train and go the extra mile in everything he does. However, that night he felt desperate due to the heat, as it was too hot to train either in or out of the garage. Texas summers are unbelievable, and no matter how many air conditioners we used, nothing was able to combat the intense heat.

Garage Training — One of Jonah's emotional breakdown moments, when he felt the intensity of the injustice and traumatic experience of training alone in the garage

Our mother sat in the corner of the garage, (where she usually sat those past four years), to cheer both of us on and give us life lessons, as she recorded our training sessions on her little camera phone. I was wiping my sweaty face and trying to stretch after a hard sparring session with Jonah, so I didn't see Jonah's face at first as he was looking down in an attempt to hide his tears. But as I looked deeper at him, I saw Jonah was in deep, silent pain. At that moment I felt Jonah's pain and frustration—it was my pain too. I heard the voice inside his head as mine kept asking the same questions, over and over again: Why us? Why do we have to suffer? What crime have we committed to deserve solitude in our garage for more than four years? Why do we have to train on our own?

Our mom was still looking down at her phone, flipping through the videos she had just taken of our training session to see which ones she would send us, so we could discuss what we should work on to improve our fighting techniques. Then, finally, in a very emotional moment, our mom raised her face and said to both of us, "Your sparring techniques are getting much better every day. I can't believe how much you both have improved."

I nodded in agreement while trying to hide my frustration with a pained smile, as I carefully stole some hidden glances at Jonah, who was still sitting on the garage floor with his head down, trying to hide his face. We both made sure not to show our weak moments to our mother. She worked hard to nurture and maintain our energized state of mind and encouraged us during these past four years of garage training, as we had no other choice after our former Master made it impossible for us to find a dojo that would agree to have us. Even though we were young, our inner strength and determination were mighty. I still feel the pain that befell me, Jonah, our mother, and our father at the hands of our former Master whose strength and connections overpowered us and weakened our desire to continue competing. Although it had only been four years of training in that small garage, and it felt like forty.

Jonah was really discouraged that day as he wanted to train in a regular gym like any other athlete. He felt wronged every time he walked inside the small garage to do his daily training sessions. Jonah remained silent and pretended to wipe his face with a small towel to hide his tears, but our mother noticed something wrong. After every practice session, he usually put on music and sang while stretching, but he was silent tonight. Mom asked Jonah to raise his head and look at her; she knew he was hiding something. Jonah was trying to hide his feelings. He didn't want our mom to feel sad as she was doing her best to make us happy. We knew how hard it was for her to sit in the garage for hours and watch us suffer during our daily training. She was trying so hard to make us happy while she was desperate for someone to cheer her up too.

Mom stood up, went to Jonah, put her hands softly on his shoulder, and asked him to look at her.

"I know how difficult this situation is for both of you, and I know you deserve better than this. I can feel your pain because it is mine too. I can imagine the amount of anger you carry within you, but I can also see God's grace in all of this. He wants you to gain knowledge and realize your abilities. He wants you to see that you can pass this test and overcome all your current obstacles. You are stronger than this situation, and I know you will overcome this challenge; you have survived training for four years in this garage on your own. Do you realize how many obstacles you have overcome so far? You are about to reach your destination. Keep your faith in God strong as He has given you the most powerful weapon to survive: your inner powers."

Our mother's conversations with us always inspired and motivated us, and I don't think we could have survived one day of this journey without her supportive, encouraging words.

Jonah looked at our mother with a stoic smile from his broken heart and gave our mom a warm hug, saying: "I wish I could talk about everything we've been through. I wish I could tell our story to children like us who suffer continually, and who face unfairness every day. I wish I could reach children who don't think they can be what they dream of and show them that they can. I hope my voice can reach children around the world to give them hope." These were Jonah's words that night and they summed up everything he felt. Jonah said what I couldn't say at that moment. Even though we were frustrated and suffered a lot, we both knew the value of the goal that awaited us —fulfilling our dream— and that it was essential we keep our faith strong, as our mom had said. We needed to stay positive and secure. We needed to keep empowering ourselves to not give up and to view our garage training as part of our journey to achieve our dreams.

After Jonah finished speaking I thought about what he had just said and I heard our mother respond, "You can let the world hear your voice." At that instant I thought this was one just another one of our mom's heartwarming teachable moments with us, but it was those words that changed our goal that day, and redirected our journey to a different path. My mom continued, 'Why not use all the journals you have written in your diary to tell your full story? You've faced many obstacles, challenges, limitations, and injustice. You can share your story with children who are in difficult situations like you. You can give them hope and explain to them how you survived. You can inspire and motivate others. Use your voice and your story to support others to be brave." These words changed our path forever.

Jonah and I wrote in our journals every night, after our training and after every competition. Writing in our diaries helped us vent all our negative feelings and express our thoughts about the situations we encountered. After our mom was done speaking, she sent us our training videos so we could sit together, as usual, and watch them to review our session, see what techniques we could improve upon, and what exercises we needed to work on. We worked to improve our performance all by ourselves.

We finished reviewing all our mom's training videos earlier that evening and sketched out a plan for the next day's training session. I wasn't sure how Jonah was feeling after speaking with our mom. Jonah seemed to want to talk, yet he looked like he was in another world. After practice, I cleaned out the garage and Jonah put the paddles and chest guards on the rack.

"Do you want to write the story with me?" Jonah asked in a deep and confident voice. I turned around and looked him firmly in the eye and said, "Yes, I do. I want to write our story with you."

That sweltering, Friday night of Summer 2020 was the first step toward embarking on a new journey that we had so desperately wanted to take for so long. That night I saw my twin brother and my one and only partner standing confident as a warrior in his armor. I saw the strong athlete, the determined kid. But, above all, I saw my role model in overcoming challenges—the bullies, the negative forces—standing on his feet ready to take on everyone causing us pain and tell the world his story, my story, our story toward defeating our obstacles and conquering our fears.

Finally, we were ready to share how we survived the isolation of more than four years in that garage, so many coaches and gyms having abandoned us for some crime we did not commit. It is our time to request answers from these coaches, not to judge them, but so that we could hear from the leaders and the masters of our sport just why they chose corruption and cowardice, over standing up for their principles; principles they claimed to teach their students.

That night the idea of writing this book was born. Our minds were focused on the numerous children who may be suffering alone. We wanted to reach those children through our words and tell them to search for strength within themselves, as we had found courage and determination in ourselves. We were eager to highlight our true story; to stand firm as we were, and declare we had weathered the storm on our own. So many people talk about mindset, positive behavior techniques, and motivation. Yet, no one has a story exactly like ours—a tale of two little kids who experienced brutal bullying and stood together against an army of obstacles.

Jonah made his way into his room and began pouring out all of his feelings and thoughts onto the blank pages; chronicling his story of pain, isolation, bullying, and rejection. I followed Jonah into his room, and we both began to recall the bitter, sad memories we had tried for so long to bury deep down. We thought if we could open our hearts freely without fear for the first time—fear of rejection or abuse—we could reach the hearts of so many children who also felt hopeless and lost. We went back to the beginning, to the first time we faced rejection and bullying —and we began to write.

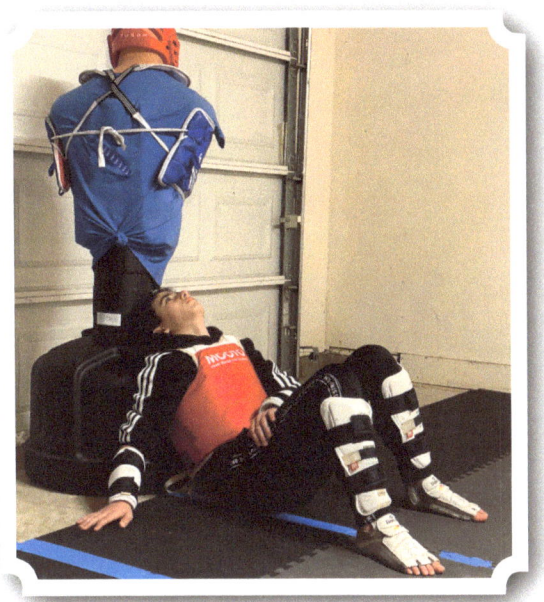

Garage Training— Jonah is drowning in deep sadness and exhaustion

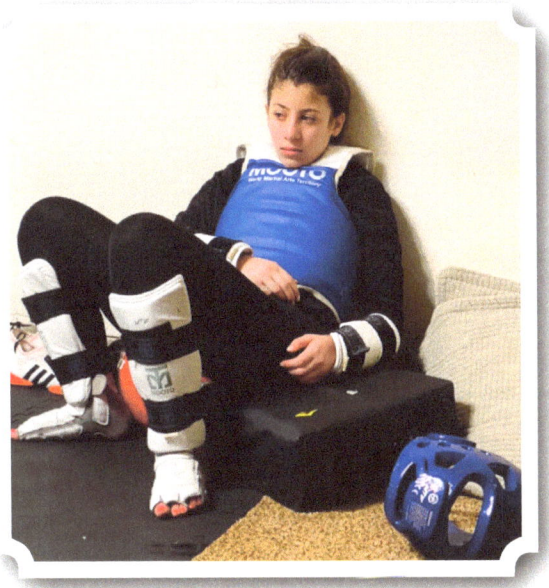

In the garage training alone — I look at Jonah and feel the injustice done to both of us, and I ask many questions about why we had to train alone in the garage all the years

Garage Training— Us after our sparring session

Garage Training — We're taking a quick break after we've finished our electronic sparring session. It was sweltering inside the garage

Garage Training— The day we decided to start writing our book, after a tough training session inside the garage

Garage Training—Jonah was sweating from the heat in the garage after a long training session

CHAPTER ONE
Introduction (Sally)

Jonah at a local tournament preparing for his Forms competition, where he presented his Blue Belt Forms

At the beginning of Summer 2012, we started the first steps of our long journey toward earning black belts in martial arts. We both began developing our love for martial arts, especially Taekwondo, at a young age, having been inspired by many fighters around the world who participated in the sport. We had read many stories about ancient warriors who fought hard with respect and discipline to bring honor to their families. It was those values behind martial arts that attracted us to learn more about this sphere of the sport. We participated in several different sports back then, but we didn't enjoy them. We played soccer, baseball, hockey, and gymnastics, (because those were the kinds of sports that most kids of our generation played), but we always felt as if we were missing something. Although we played on several teams and participated in many competitions, our involvement in these sports lacked purpose.

Teamwork was one of the common principles in these sports. We were supposed to learn many great things through playing sports, such as developing skills to communicate with our teammates, exchanging ideas, and building positive, supportive techniques as members of the team. However, we have always been struck by the fact that talking about principles in these sports is one thing, but demonstrating them on the field is another. Even when I (Sally) was involved in gymnastics, the unbalanced competition between team members was driving me away from the sport. In fact, we both were unable to find our identities or purpose while playing these other sports. We knew there was a more meaningful foundation behind these competitive sports apart from competing with others, or against others, but we couldn't find it. We thought we might be the problem. Our potential toward mastery in these kinds of sports just didn't reach the level we wanted because the rejection and manipulation by others made our passion fade away; it destroyed our desire to keep trying, and made our motivation to continue going forward dim.

We gradually began to withdraw from participation in these sports after realizing we were being rejected not because of our abilities, but because of our identity, and due to the racial, ethnic, and religious prejudices of others. Unfortunately, we couldn't change other people's opinions and perceptions of us, so we gave up trying to be the best in order to impress others.

We began to develop an interest in martial arts—not as a sport, but as a way to express our inner selves. We were eager to discover our identities and to find our passions. Regrettably, although we were young, racism had affected us early. It was not clearly visible, but we felt it through the looks of others and their behavior toward us. The most distressing emotion a child goes through is feeling rejected and unwelcome — not because of their personality or thoughts but because of something the child can't control. Sadly, we weren't able to recognize the motives behind this unreasonable rejection until later on.

Our elementary school years were our worst school years. We could not imagine that kids our age would have to experience this much negativity. Our peers were young like us—happy, playful, and full of energy. At the time, we couldn't understand why some kids weren't so nice to us, but were nice to others. Why did they bully us? Why didn't they want to play with us?

As we grew, the negative feelings toward us grew as well. Everything around us was unclear as we tried to understand what caused some of our peers to act the way they did toward us. We encountered the term "stereotype" early on. Other people's negative perceptions of us, our race, and our ethnicity were the beginning of an unpleasant campaign of continuous rejection. Born in the United States to Arab parents—both of whom were well educated and respected in Israel—who immigrated more than 25 years ago from Israel to pursue their dream, we were still rejected by our peers simply because of who we were.

The silent rejection that accompanied us throughout our elementary years was like a deadly cancer slowly spreading through our bodies; while our smiling faces tried to hide the terrible pain pressing down on our hearts. Having been introduced to negativity at a very young age, we were lonely and had low self-esteem. However, what saved us was the overall positivity that our mother nurtured inside us which served as a protective shield for our mental health.

We were blessed with a mother who was our shadow. She had a certain magic, a positive spirit, that allowed us to put away all the hurtful, angry, and sad feelings we had developed during the school day. She miraculously eliminated any negative emotions we were experiencing and boosted us up to remain the way we had to be. She encouraged us to believe in ourselves and to forgive. In fact, forgiveness was a panacea for us as it allowed us to repair our scars and make each day a fresh start—a fresh start to allow our peers to get to know us better. We tried hard to represent who we were. We wanted to stay on the right path—to forgive, heal our souls, and attract positive forces into our lives. Our mother was careful to remind us daily that forgiveness was the only remedy we needed to stay healthy.

Our love for martial arts increased day by day as we were inspired by the stories of people fighting for a purpose. We, too, felt that we had a purpose, but we couldn't figure out what it was at the time. We were young and couldn't express ourselves in a way that would allow our parents to view martial arts as we saw it.

Our parents were like many other parents who were willing to do anything they could so that their children would excel at sports. Although they personally had no passion for playing or viewing sports, they went the extra mile to allow us to join many sports teams. We both played soccer together when we were kids, but later on, each of us joined different sports teams. Jonah liked kicking the ball a lot. It was part of his personality, he loved to run and chase the ball. Jonah wanted to be free, and I think in soccer he found a way to release that energy. He ran non-stop without getting tired. I didn't understand what kind of joy he felt while running, but I began to realize as I got older that Jonah was trying to escape his pain. He was running away from the social rejection he had to face at a young age.

While Jonah was trying to find a way to express his feelings, I was different in the way I chose to express mine. I didn't realize at the time that I needed to fill my *social* passion. From a young age, I had developed a defense mechanism. I don't know if it was something I was born with or something unconsciously developed inside me. I did not tolerate others easily, so the rejection we experienced did not hurt me to the same degree as it did Jonah. Jonah is a pure angel, with a heart full of love that can cover the whole planet. He is peaceful, respectful, kind, and gentle. So, even though he was hurt badly, he was always forgiving. Even though things weren't good for either of us in sports, we were committed. We continued to play recreational sports and repeatedly tried to join teams from our community, where parents create the teams and one parent is the coach.

Since our teammates were the same peers from school who had rejected us, we were not welcomed onto any of these teams. We were not told anything explicitly, but their attitudes toward us made it obvious. If we stood by them in the field, they would not pass the ball to us, and they certainly would not invite us to their parties. Although we wouldn't understand until we were older why we were being treated that way, that this prejudice wasn't directed to us as individuals, but rather the race and ethnicity we represented. We didn't let this exclusion get us down. We maintained the same attitude with the same positive reaction to every unpleasant event we encountered, never allowing these negative forces to define us. We decided instead to focus on one goal: our academic excellence.

Our mother's daily motivational words inspired us: "Your education is your power. You need to be educated, and through knowledge, you will make a change for you and many children like you. Others' perceptions of you are their own; they have never been true, and they will not define you. Don't let anyone dim the light within you; follow your mind and control your feelings. Always forgive because, through forgiveness, you will be healed."

After disappointing experiences playing on traditional recreational sports teams, we started going to Taekwondo classes, as none of our peers practiced this sport. This was a way to escape our bullies. Unfortunately, we couldn't stop their pathetic laughter at us because we didn't play any "great sports" like they did. We weren't part of the "cool kids" who would talk about their sports games and tournaments as part of the classroom discussions in elementary school. I wasn't one of the "popular girls" who loved to dance or cheer. Jonah and I were both martial arts kids. We participated in a sport that no one else in our school played, therefore no one cared to hear about it. Although Taekwondo was an Olympic sport, none of our schoolmates or even some elementary school teachers saw it as a legitimate sport. They saw us as losers who failed to join a "real" sports team.

I still remember our elementary school years. How could I forget? It was a painful experience for both of us. Jonah wasn't allowed to play with the boys who were playing soccer at recess time because he wasn't part of any sports team. At the same time, a group of girls who were practicing gymnastics and dance were repeatedly calling me fat. It got to the point where they didn't even want to take a picture with me. I will never forget that feeling. We both carried a heavy pain on our fragile backs. Yet, it wasn't the fault of our peers; it was the fault of society. We live in a society that encourages stereotypes. Knowledge of other sports was not provided to our peers at that time. Respect for different sports and other cultures was also not taught. Many other children who were not part of a "popular sport" were victims of numerous acts of bullying. The community encouraged these acts by giving significant, unbalanced prestige to the children who played certain sports. It was as if the whole world revolved around those sports alone. But what about swimming, fencing, tennis, snowboarding, and many other sports out there?

We started to educate others about Taekwondo—providing information about it during our show-and-tell days at school, talking about it if we were students of the week, or through the posters we made. We found opportunities to show our peers and teachers that Taekwondo is a well-known, well-esteemed and, most notably, an Olympic sport. Although our efforts to amplify the beauty of our sport did not change anyone's perceptions of it, we were able to feel the honor of being Taekwondo athletes. In fact, the older we got, the more we loved and committed to our sport. It was the values that were held behind the black belt and the principles that shone through the brightest white of our uniforms that attracted us. We studied Taekwondo, researched our sport, and read many books about the mind and body connection to understand our sport. Reading was our salvation.

Our journey toward black belts in Taekwondo has been rich in knowledge. We believe that the rejection we experienced played an essential role in amplifying our love for this sport. We may have been rejected because others saw us differently, but we did not let their rejection defeat us. We used it as motivation to find our purpose and to demonstrate that stereotypes never define who someone is. Stereotypes develop through a process of irrational perceptions by some people and then spread to others. We transformed the rejection of ourselves and our sport into a positive boost that made us yearn for success later in life. Obtaining our black belts has taken five years of continuous training and commitment. During that time, we continued to face harder things than most people our age, but redirected that energy into achieving our goals.

Finding our identities was not an easy thing to do. We have been through many struggles that have tested our mental capacity and challenged our patience. Sadly, the opinions that our peers and some members in the elementary school community have of us and our sport have not changed. We still suffer from a lack of respect for participating in a sport that is not seen as "cool." However, we have remained determined to reach the international level and prove that we are the only ones who can define ourselves. We have dedicated our time to enriching our minds with knowledge through the challenges and obstacles we face, sharpening our identities, and developing a long-term vision toward achieving the goals we intend to overcome and the dreams we want to make happen. Strengthening our mindset and shaping our identities was our ultimate goal.

Me at a local tournament practicing my Green belt Forms, before I enters the mat to compete

Us at a local tournament where we won titles in a forms belt competition— Jonah was a blue-green belt, and I was an orange-green belt

At our first opening in Las Vegas — We competed in the blue belt forms and sparring competition

We are in our first color belt National Championship— We still haven't gotten our black belts yet

CHAPTER TWO
Lost Identity (Jonah)

Identity. Who are we? Our behaviors, our dreams, and the way the world views us. Identity is what makes us who we are; it is a reflection of our principles, values, beliefs, attitudes, thoughts, and behavior. Identity is a unique trait that varies from person to person. Identity is created throughout our lives by the many situations we go through and the various challenges we face. Regrettably, some people allow the circumstances of their external environment to overly influence the formation of their identity, giving those characteristics too much weight. At the same time, others take control of the amount of external influence on their identification. As a result, they go through obstacles and face many confrontations to create their own identities and forge their own path. The nature of a person's identity is a choice. We choose our identity based on our interactions and reactions to the many challenges and events we face during our lives.

We were among those who refused to shape their identity based on the opinions of others. We refused to be ordinary and went above and beyond to form our identities. We rejected the stereotypes that others put on us. We refused to be labeled with titles that did not represent us, our thoughts, or our feelings. Throughout our journey, we have been searching for our lost identity—the one that was scared to be seen, scarred from rejection. We have gone through many twists and turns that put us on many difficult paths to finding the true "I am" behind the mask others wanted us to wear. Through these experiences, we have realized that the conditions in which we live—our surroundings, our environment, and the people who doubt us or do not believe in us—will never define who we are. Our personal experiences may help shape us, but in the end, we define who we are through the process we progressed through these experiences. The way we react to challenges, the changes we go through, and the obstacles we face define the true "me" within each one of us.

We have faced many obstacles that made us who we are today and what we want to be later in the future.

My Life at The Dojo (Jonah)

We spent our elementary school years trying to avoid any negativity. We focused on forming our own identities—not the ones that other people wanted us to have, but the ones we were happy to embody. We gradually began to exclude other sports from our daily physical activities and focused on the only sport we believed in. However, Sally continued to practice gymnastics in addition to Taekwondo, dividing her time between the two sports. After her daily three-hour gymnastics training, she immediately headed to the dojo to do Taekwondo training. She was strong. She never appeared tired and never complained. Sally was a role model for many dojo athletes, including myself.

Our Taekwondo journey toward our black belts was long, requiring daily lessons, including on the weekends. We took advantage of every opportunity and advantage the dojo offered. We loved Taekwondo very much and wanted to do our best to succeed.

Things went smoothly for the first two months of our black belt journey, until things changed at the dojo. Our initial coach quit so we were automatically reassigned to the dojo's headmaster and owner. We had never had a class with him before, as we were only at the intermediate level and he taught the seniors and the competition team. He seemed nice to us, and he made the lessons fun instead of serious. I felt he wanted to attract kids my age to stay because Taekwondo was not a popular sport. I was focused on my training and respectful of my Master. In return, the Master started showing an interest in my work ethic and invited me to join the Master's program, which was only offered to elite athletes of the dojo. It was a great opportunity for me to show my leadership skills and I began spending hours at the dojo helping younger kids learn the different forms of the sport.

Sally, on the other hand, wasn't having such an easy time. She was still balancing gymnastics and training at the dojo, but lamentably, her time at gymnastics was very challenging. She was being bullied by a group of girls who attended the same school we did, and that, in spite of her love for the sport, made her feel negatively about the gym. Our mother informed the gym owner of what was going on, but because there were so many athletes and the gym was so large, the coaches couldn't keep up with what was going on between the girls during training. Fortunately, Sally's time at the dojo was much more positive. It didn't take long for the both of us to join the competition team, by invitation of the Master who saw something in us. It was a huge achievement for both of us, especially in front of our peers at school who grievously only increased their bullying.

The Competition Team Journey (Jonah)

Our mission changed the moment we joined the competition team; even though we were ultimately searching for our overall purpose in life, we found ourselves focusing on our next competitions. The team competition was different from recreational training. We were training with many athletes who were older than us and had more advanced ranked belts than us. Saturdays were team sparring days. We would attend sparring sessions with these athletes, without regard to massive differences in height, age, belt rank, or weight division. In spite of this, it was the most enjoyable time for me. I loved sparring and challenging myself to improve my skills, so much so, that I didn't give much weight to the huge differences between the seniors in our team and me. Sally had a different story, however. She hesitated kicking other athletes and sometimes cried because of it. Finally, after a long time, she started to develop a sense of excitement for competition, especially as she started working on building her self-confidence when we trained alone in our house.

You would think that our achievement would bring us closer to our peers, but it did not. We started noticing that some of our teammates, those who were closer in age, had changed their behavior toward us, especially when we won our matches in the local competitions we attended with the team. They started staying away from us and avoided talking to us.

Things started to worsen when the team's groups developed, and we were left out. We thought "here we go again," as it felt too familiar from our previous sports experiences. Nobody wanted to be our partners, and kids our age on the team started complaining about our performance, how hard we kicked, and said that they couldn't train with us. Therefore, Sally and I had to train together all the time. We became partners in training and competition as well. We began to improve and develop fighting techniques. Our fighting style attracted the parents there. We become known in the dojo for our disciplined techniques and skill. We focused on developing our techniques and ignored the irrational, negative feelings toward us.

At that time, the dojo's headmaster went through a family crisis that affected his judgment, professionalism, and behavior at the dojo. He became more aggressive and continually expressed his anger toward the team. He was always mad, he yelled a lot, and was suspicious of any behavior. We started to develop anxiety and fear toward him, as some of the younger kids were punished for simple mistakes. The dojo became a nightmare for everyone on the competition team.

In spite of the scary environment in the dojo, we became dominant and focused only on our mission. Our commitment to our mission was getting stronger day by day. Parents looked at us and started to pressure their kids to work harder. A split began to emerge between team members, and the Master did nothing to reunite the team. Unfortunately, the Master liked division and began using it to create a competitive appetite among team members. He seemed to enjoy watching what was happening and even appeared satisfied seeing team members insult each other during sparring sessions.

Competitiveness among team members started to go beyond the sparring sessions. It started to provoke negativity within the squad on top of the negative attitude the Master already showed toward the team. In fact, things only got worse at the dojo. After the Master's family crisis came to a sad ending, he began to unleash his anger on us and bully us for no reason. He told us that was how he would teach us discipline. The morale of the team just kept getting worse.

Bullying is a Sickness (Jonah)

The team members observed our Master and his actions as he was the role model. Since he was angry and treated others badly, the others began to copy his behavior. However, parents continued to complain about their children showing a lack of respect for our Master. What they didn't realize is that the team members would never have respect for someone who took a negative approach to teaching; someone who allowed aggression and bullying.

Our mother was our shadow: where we went, she went—not because she didn't trust us, but to protect and guide us. She always told us to show compassion and empathy for others, even if they offended us. We tried to stay positive and remain patient. Going to the dojo became a challenge for us. We started to have to separate our feelings from our training. We tried to be rational and not emotional about what we encountered. We understood that the bullying was not our fault, but a consequence of outside forces we could not control. Parents would drop their kids off at the gym and come back to pick them up at the end of each training session; while our mom was the only parent sitting and watching our training—something that made our Master uncomfortable. He didn't like the idea of our mother observing his aggressive behavior toward the team. He was a completely different person in the recreational classes, where parents spent less than an hour watching their children during form classes. We began noticing his aggression toward us, and he started attacking us because our mom was sitting and witnessing his unstable behavior all the time.

Aggression is a dangerous feeling that contains anger, sadness, hatred, and rejection. It can harm the person holding it, as well as the people they encounter. The aggressive behaviors of our former Master were increasing day by day, and his behaviors affected most of the young athletes in our gym. Everyone cultivated feelings of fear and anxiety toward him; some gave up, but many became copies of him. Our mother had to speak to the Master regarding this matter and explained to him that his aggression affected our well-being. The Master took offense at our mother's remarks, thinking she had invaded his territory as a coach. He didn't like this move and accused her of coaching us. A wide door of pain opened at that moment, as our Master changed his gym policy by indirectly encouraging our other teammates to start bullying us. His vanity blinded his vision as a coach and his professionalism as a Master.

While our journey began with pain, it was ultimately a journey toward self-discovery.

Pain Breeds Motivation (Jonah)

Bullying both at practice and at school forced Sally to quit gymnastics. Dealing with bullying in school, at the gym, unexplained aggression, and rejection in the dojo—How could we cope with all this? We were young and just starting to see life. Would our lives always be like this? Is what is happening to us normal? There were many questions we asked our mother in hopes of getting rid of our pain.

Our mother always comforted us and told us stories of real people who had faced many challenges and rejections because they were different. She told us: "You have to accept that life is not easy; to achieve your goals, you have to face trials and difficulties, and you have to accept that many will stand in your way because you are different from them. This does not mean that you are wrong or that they are wrong. We are all different in many ways, but we will have peaceful and healed minds when we agree to accept other people's differences."

We knew that we needed to learn to adapt to any situation we faced, even if it was painful. We could not continue to run from obstacles or rejection. We had to start developing techniques to teach ourselves how to adapt to any obstacle. We must do as our mom advised us: "Escaping the obstacles you face by simply changing your paths will not solve your problem, and will never get you to your desired destination. Don't let this fear of rejection and the pain from the obstacles you encounter stop you from being the best version of yourselves."

This was our mother's daily motivational pep talk, and we trusted her. Her calm demeanor had always reinforced the importance of positivity in our lives. We knew she was right: running away from our bullies would never stop them from bullying us. Turning our backs on any obstacles or challenges we run into would never teach us how to reach our goals, nor would it help us achieve them. We needed to be strong enough to handle all the negative forces thrown at us, and we had to learn to forgive and move on. Forgiveness brings healing, and through healing we can restore our positive energy. A peaceful mind will give us a clear view and enhance our focus on the tasks ahead.

It wasn't an easy road, after all, we were just kids. How could our brains be expected to comprehend the size of obstacles we were facing? How could we raise our maturity to reach the highest levels of professionalism? Why do we have to go through this? All we wanted to do was to practice and learn a sport that we chose and loved so much. But the pressure of rejection, along with pressure from trying to find our identities and overcome our abilities were beyond the capabilities of young minds.

CHAPTER THREE
The Beginning (Jonah)

Sally and I started our local Color Belt competitions

Our painful story began in 2016, the year we started lining up to enter the competitive world stage of Taekwondo. Before that, we lived in a bubble full of lies on account of our "perfect" coach. Our Master told us to respect, obey, and demonstrate responsibility and leadership, but that was only an illusion. We are told to love what we do, and we did. We were living our dream, holding on to that dream, as we waited for the chance to enter the competitive ring where we could show respect, integrity, honesty, and our love for our sport—a sport based on principles and driven by legends for thousands of years.

We still remember the first time our mom took us to the dojo in 2012. We were so excited and happy to start the first lesson of a sport we loved even before we began participating in it. We felt mentally prepared to begin our first sparring session. On that day, not only did we realize that we had taken our first step in our first Taekwondo lesson, but we understood we were also taking our initial step on an unknown, and ultimately painful, journey that took more than eight years, and still continues today. It was a journey that killed our childhood and made us mentally mature before we were physically mature. This was not the kind of trip we wanted to take. It was a trip forced upon us by our Master whose goal was to clip our wings so that we could no longer fly.

The Inner Conflict (Jonah)

We were young, excited, and anxious to succeed. We knew that with practice we would improve, capture our moment, find our identity, and soar to the heights of our potential. However, the identity we wanted to have was not what others wanted us to have. Our identity was not created by the stereotypes others held toward us, nor by perceptions of our culture. Our identity is a product of our thoughts, personalities, values, and experiences. It is a creation of the journeys we take throughout our lives that develop our identities.

Our coach had a different point of view than us. Unfortunately, he always believed in his opinion alone, causing many dreams to die before they sprouted. He contended that if we failed it was because we were not good enough to be champions. Our Master believed that if we failed, it would shame him and cause him to be blacklisted, which led him to humiliate and abuse us.

We told ourselves that we would not be the people he imagined us to be. We would not fail because of his aggression, and we would not allow him to control our minds. Therefore, to avoid this situation we had to win our competitions; we had to win for ourselves and not for him. We understood this was our battle, and we needed to win no matter what we faced, or the degree of pain we endure throughout the journey. But how were we to win while living through this horrible abuse? Should we tell our parents of our fear? Did we really have the courage to engage in battle with our Master? We chose this sport, yet we were sure that it was not the same as the one we were introduced to through the mythical stories we read.

During this time, Sally began to develop a sense of rebellion toward everything we encountered in the dojo. She encouraged me to stand up for myself and talk to our Master about how I feel. But how we could talk to our Master while he covers us with a dark cloud that fills our hearts with fear and shame? How could we stand up to a man who always disrespects us, finds ways to humiliate us, imitate us, and continually makes fun of us in front of the class. In spite of the verbal abuse, and because respect is one of the principles of our sport, we decided to continue to show our Master deference. Even after our mom spoke to our Master several times, he showed no interested in changing. Nevertheless, we respected him, because that is what martial artists do.

Patience Is Power (Jonah)

The national championship was knocking at our door. This championship is where we fought for a position on the national team. We desperately wanted to win on the national stage to show our Master that we could win. We wanted our coach to stop punishing us. We wanted this nightmare of repeated abuse to end, and we wanted to enjoy participating in the sport we love while enjoying a positive, encouraging environment. We were eager to show our elementary school classmates that we weren't the losers they kept calling us. We lived with two conflicting pressures: (1) our desire to stand up for ourselves, even if we didn't realize how to do so; and (2) our desire to slap rejection in the face and win—and with that, end all the constant pain growing inside of us. Because of the peer rejection, the unrealistic stereotypes about us, our teammates' negative feelings toward us, and, most importantly, our Master's abuse we had to face many battles, and the only solution to winning those battles was a national victory.

Going to the national championship was expensive. Training fees, airline tickets, hotels, and food expenses had to be covered. The AAU Nationals were in Florida, and to prepare for Nationals, we had to spend all our summer training intensively, forgetting about vacations, playtime, and downtime. We trained three times every day.

Our daily schedule was to alternate between sleeping, eating, and training. While our peers went to fun summer camps or traveled, we trained daily, working on managing our weight, and focusing on one goal to succeed in our mission and win. We needed to win to build our identity; to show our bullies that they were wrong about us. We needed to win and invest extraordinary mental and physical efforts to achieve our goal beyond our expectations.

Living under the pressure of training and focusing on our dream wasn't easy, but we believed in that dream. Although this stressful situation was excruciating for us, we tried to make every minute of the suffering and the process of arriving at our destination enjoyable. We imagined ourselves on the winner's podium and loved the feeling. It is painful to give everything you have to your dream only to have your ruthless Master crush that ambition by planting seeds of fear and doubt within you.

We will never forget the look our Master gave us when we walked into the ring. We were terrorized by him, as he was determined to instill doubt inside our heads about our abilities. As kids, we were not capable of programming our minds to think professionally at that moment. We couldn't separate our feelings from our thoughts. He was our Master, our coach, the one who was supposed to comfort us, encourage us, look us in the eyes, and tell us, "I trust you. You can do it. You can win." We longed to hear these words from him, and we still had hope in him. But, unfortunately, we both lost. How could we win when we entered the arena full of doubt and fear? We weren't afraid of the competition or our opponent, but of our Master's reaction.

We couldn't change or move to another dojo. Our Master was so powerful that he was able to destroy many years of hard work by telling other dojos not to accept us. This is what he told our mother when she raised the option of switching dojos for our well-being and mental health. Our Master indirectly sent her the message that if we left his dojo he would ensure we never practiced our sport again. He said that none of the local dojos would accept us because they wouldn't be able to accept a former athlete from another Master; that was the agreement between coaches. This is part of the political aspect of our sport, where masters and coaches can use their power for anything that benefits them, even if it destroys athletes' dreams, careers, and reputations.

We lost, and our wings were broken even before they opened for flight. The thought of going back to the dojo after our defeats and knowing exactly what we were going to face when we got there was terrifying to both of us.

When we got back to training, our Master was very angry with all the athletes at the National Championship because we had lost. He was captivated by his ego and never allowed us to explain and discuss what happened in the ring. He had always said that if we lose, it's because we are losers, and because we don't listen to him—and this is exactly what happened that day. We took what we had to from him, and we felt devastated, humiliated, and emotionally hurt. We listened to his words telling us that we are losers and that we would never achieve anything in life. While he belittled and disparaged us, we were busy telling ourselves that this was not the end. We would continue our fight, refusing to surround ourselves with his negativity. We would work harder than before to achieve the victory we dreamed about—not for him or our bullies, but for us.

Our Master continued to abuse us mentally and emotionally. He divided the team and sowed hatred among the team's members, a technique he used to control us all and make us compete ruthlessly against each other. This was the beginning of a painful era because of him. He started ignoring some of the athletes, praising some, and insulting others. He even built social relationships with some parents and talked about others behind their backs. The team's divide began to spread out from the athletes to their parents, and parents started taking sides and forming factions.

The loss at Nationals was considered an insult to our Master, his reputation, and his position as the National team coach. Our Master was very strong and had connections that convinced us to keep us silent about his verbal emotional abuse and harassment. Besides, who would have believed us if we opened out mouths against him? Who would stand by us and fight for us? It was a dead-end, but this would have been the end for us if we had tried to say anything.

Our mother kept coming to our daily practice at the dojo, encouraging us with her eyes and her smile. She was not allowed to say anything, even though she tried several times to question how our Master treated us. Dismissal was the only way our Master dealt with many of our mother's questions over his treatment of us. He repeatedly accused her of coaching us and pushing into an area she wasn't supposed to enter. Over and over again, he would present her with hundreds reasons why he should lead us on this crucial path that he called "discipline." Although our mother never approved of what our coach was doing, nevertheless, she continued to attend our daily training sessions, never leaving the dojo's front office room where she would watch us through the glass window; looking at us lovingly, and telling us with her eyes not to be afraid to complete our training.

Our father also began to come to the dojo, after our mother told him how differently our Master treated us. She was worried about our mental health and our self-confidence. Once our father saw the Master's abusive treatment of us, our parents decided that they couldn't keep us under our Master's supervision any longer, to continue to suffer his verbal and emotional abuse. Our parents decided that we needed to move on to another dojo with another master— and even if no one wanted to accept us, we would find a private coach to train us for competition next year at the national level.

Sally and I felt unsure about moving dojos, not because we wanted to stay with our Master, but because we were worried about the national championship. Our Master was the national team's head coach, and we knew that he could destroy our chances of success even if we had a private coach. We had no doubt he could find a way to prevent us from participating. We heard him talk with pride many times about the athletes and coaches that came before him who had stood against him and failed. We couldn't continue training in this scary environment, worrying all the time about each movement we took and facing such negative forces. We never blamed our teammates for their negative approach to us because we understood that bullying is a learned behavior. They were young; they learned to be bullies by observing our Master. It was the only expected way to express their negative and jealous feelings toward us.

Jealousy is a natural feeling that develops when others are unable to reach their goals, succeed, or achieve their dream while watching others succeed. We understood the negative behavior of our teammates toward us but could not do anything about their behavior, other than ignoring them and concentrate on achieving our goal. Focusing on something positive was the only solution to all the negative forces and distractions being thrown our way at the time.

Our Master realized how serious our parents were about their decision to remove us from the dojo. His ego could not accept the loss of students, especially us. He claimed to our parents that his approach is the way many martial arts are practiced worldwide, and that his methods follow old-school rules that make students mentally stronger. Our parents strongly disagreed with him and insisted on moving us. They respectfully asked him to speak to one of his colleagues and make the transfer peacefully with respect on all sides. After a long discussion, our Master explained to our parents that none of the local Taekwondo schools would take us because they would not be willing to cross him. Therefore, our parents had no other choice but to give our Master one last chance, because the national championship was around the corner. The decision to stay was a tough one for my family, but our Master had not left us any choice. How could we throw away years of hard work and give up on our dream to make the national team? So, we decided to stay and accept his terms, even though it was a painful choice. We felt achieving our dream was worth the pain.

National training started, and along with it, our Master started his new technique: ignoring us. It was an incredibly traumatic experience for us as children. Every day we headed to practice knowing what lay ahead. He began letting us practice on the side, ignoring that we were even in the dojo. He stopped talking to us and became more ruthless than ever. It was a horrific experience filled with extreme discrimination, racism, and emotional abuse. It killed our passion for training.

Our team members—seniors, juniors, and cadets—had sparring sessions every night during our national training. These sparring sessions became a nightmare for us as our Master started using our teammates to punish us. He picked the team members he knew didn't like us or didn't talk to us, and these athletes tried to hit us in every possible way they could. Sparring sessions became a matter of life or death for us. We had to fight whoever our coach chose for us regardless of size, weight, or age, and they were fighting to hurt us physically and emotionally.

At the time, we were dropping weight to be in the 10-11-year-old weight division. We trained three times a day and during the weekends. We were so focused on winning nationals, as that was our ticket to freedom. We needed to be on the national team so we could leave our Master for good. That's what we thought would give us some relief and would end his abuse, but we were wrong.

Knowing and witnessing how our Master used our teammates to punish us when we asked to leave his dojo was a sad reality we had to face and accept. Our effort to avoid arguments with our teammates and concentrate on our training, our dream, and our goal was difficult for two children who were not yet 11 years old. We were sure it wasn't our teammates' fault as their minds were poisoned and clouded by the intense darkness of constant conversations and behaviors that our Master imposed daily. Yet, the more pressure we had, the more determined we were to achieve our goals nationwide. It was a path full of torture, pain, and injustice. It was like we were stuck inside a maze and had to keep running and searching for the exit.

Every day we were developing physically, but we were also growing mentally, getting stronger in large part due to our parents' unwavering support. They encouraged us, motivated us, and reminded us why we chose to move forward despite this misery. They would both accompany us to every training session, waiting in the front office room or outside the dojo looking at us through the glass windows and filling our hearts with hope and motivation. The moments when our eyes met those of our mother's nourished us. Through her eyes, we began to see a way to victory and a way to put an end to our endless pain.

We remember how our dad would leave work early to follow our night practice session, smile at us with a calm smile, and silently communicate to us how proud he was of us. We would train courageously, while dealing with our Masters' divisive behavior, humiliation, and ignorance. We knew it was now about more than just winning nationals. Our story with him had just begun, even though it was bitter and painful. Our Master thought we were weak and would easily fall apart. He believed that if he ignored us, he would successfully kill our passion. Yes, indeed, he had won his first fight with us, but after a short time we gathered our strength and redirected our focus toward our primary goal. We didn't lose during those sparring sessions. In fact, Sally developed into the Iron Woman of the dojo and became both mentally and physically stronger.

Our growth did not stop there; our powerful will to win the national championship and join the national team increased each and every day. Our love for Taekwondo filled our hearts and ran through out veins; something that set us apart from our teammates. We tried to maintain a positive attitude for the last few days leading up the competition, honestly fighting, while respecting the principles of the sport we had loved from day one.

We read everything we could about Taekwondo, enriching our minds with the origin, history, stories, and legends of the sport. The more we read, the more fire inside us to win grew. We ignored every agonizing kick we took from our teammates; we took every criticism our Master gave us and redirected our eyes toward the goal we had set for ourselves. We were focused and channeled all the negative emotions into motivation. We did precisely what our mother told us to do: forgive so that we could heal. Forgiveness was our medicine at the time, and it was very effective.

Dallas-Fort Worth International Airport Terminal (July 5, 2016, 5:48 a.m.)
On our way to the AUU/USA National Championships, Fort Lauderdale, Florida

The clock was ticking toward the national championship, and finally, the day we had been waiting for finally arrived. On the morning of July 7, 2016, our mother woke us up while we slept in a hotel room in Fort Lauderdale, Florida, where the tournament was being held. She was smiling and full of energy. Her face reflected calm, and she spread her joy by talking to us. We clearly remember her speaking to us; her voice resonating inside our ears and her words living in our hearts. She looked into our eyes and, in a soft voice, said:

> *"Listen carefully; you need to know one thing before you step into the ring today and before your matches begin. We live in a world that revolves around social acceptance, and you have to understand the psychology behind success in this world. When you are able to understand that no one has the power to spread negative energy inside you, no one has the power to question you, and no one can stand against you, you will be undefeated. That moment you reach self-realization you will know what matters most to you. So, don't worry about the acceptance of others, and don't wait for social approval for everything you do—don't let your happiness be tied to social approval. The moment you do that, you will lose your identity and your self-respect. Remember that these negative behaviors of others toward you are all like emojis. The emojis are subject to change according to the current situation or according to the needs of others from you.*
>
> *Don't change who you really are to fit the group. Groups, friends, and teammates change daily when there are conflicts of interest. Emojis act as an emotional response mechanism to help express other people's feelings toward you, your situations, and the events in which you participate. Emojis cannot change facts about the event or about you. Be yourself, even if you have to stand alone.*
>
> *The moment you begin to differentiate yourself from negative thoughts or the perceptions of others is the moment when you will be who you want to be and begin to attract positivity. That will be the real version of you and your abilities. At that moment, you will clearly see who you are, what you want to be, and what your goals and dreams are. At that moment, you can start communicating easily with your powers. This power is within you, and only you can bring it out.*

Discover your inner strength today and find out exactly why you are here and why you want to win. Ask yourself, do you want to win to prove your Master wrong? Do you want to win to impress him? Do you want to win to gain his respect and stop his negativity toward you? Or, do you want to win to earn respect for yourself, the love of the sport, the hard work you put in all these years to realize your dream and your identity? Know exactly what your goal is and what you've learned from your traumatic experiences.

When you enter the ring today, enter it with a mission to revive your identity. Fight for the love of sports and fight with pleasure, not with hate. Enjoy your abilities and talent and enjoy your competition. Treat your opponent with respect and spread positivity around you because you grow and win only through positivity.

Most importantly, block your ears from any negative comments from your Master and try to separate yourself from his toxic words. Believe that if he didn't see something powerful coming from within you, your talent, and strong determination, he wouldn't fight you the way he does. Bring the strength within you to life and make your final year of youth competition an unforgettable one."

This speech forever changed our perception of life.

National Championship, August 2016 (Jonah)

Sally started her fight early that morning. She was extremely excited about the competition, but she was also very calm. As Sally entered the ring with our Master behind her, I looked at our mother to ask her to pray for Sally. Our mother sat away from the ring, while all of our teammates gathered around waiting to see Sally lose the match. I went to our mother and wondered why she wasn't standing up and cheering for Sally as usual. I looked at her face as I approached her, and she was smiling softly at me. I stood in front of her and told her to come to stand by the ringside with me and encourage Sally. Our mother gently told me that Sally no longer needed any more encouragement or cheering because she had found her inner strength. She knew why she wanted to win her fights, and she would shine.

I didn't get it at the time, but after that day I realized what my mom meant by those words. Sally looked different in the ring. Her face was serious, reflecting a strength and confidence I had never seen before. She started fighting with determination and masterfully earned her points. Sally won her matches one by one, standing in the ring like a lion who sought to declare that arena her kingdom. She was fighting alone while our Master's face was changing colors. His eyes were moving in different directions with confusion, even though he was trying to look normal.

I watched my twin sister as she took a step toward a certain future. Her eyes were focused on her goal, and her mind was clear. Sally truly fought like a lion, roaring loudly to awaken the beast within her. Finally, after four tough matches, she declared victory, spread her wings, and soared. At that moment, I turned to look back at our mother who was still sitting in her seat, eyes closed, lips softly moving. Our mother was quietly praying.

Our mom has always had a strong relationship with God. She trusted Him and always believed in His abilities. She walked toward me confidently, looked me in the eyes, and as she was about to hug me, she whispered softly in my ear, *"Now is the time to let out the strength within you."* I looked at my mother's face. Her lips continued whispering to me, *"Fight bravely, let the fear go away, and don't forget why you really want to win. Let the love of your sport lead your battles and make your victory a graveyard for the negativity that was trying to diminish your dream."* I nodded my head confidently and gave my mother a warm kiss, while asking her to continue praying for me. As I was hugging my mother, feeling her love and warmth, I silently prayed: *"God, stay with me. Plant the seeds of faith within me, and help me fly like my sister Sally."*

Sally is in the ring, ready to start her fights in the AAU/USA National Championship/FL

National Championship, July 2016. After winning all her matches and taking the gold medal, Sally became a Team AAU/USA member

The Awakeness (Jonah)

My fight began with a different spirit. I wanted to win for myself and not for my Master. I wanted to fight my last fight with honor, respect, and love for the game. I wanted to be the last one standing, and I wanted to show myself that I could win, not for a medal or status on the national team, but to prove that I possessed the principles upon which my sport was built.

My first fight ended with a gap (20-point) lead over an opponent who had beat me over the past two years. At that moment, I felt something different; I felt the smallness of my Master. I glanced at him and saw his eyes rolling to the right and left, as if he intended to avoid looking at me. I wondered what was going on inside his head at that moment. He didn't say a word to me throughout the fight, and it seemed to me that he was indeed ignoring me.

My Master thought that by ignoring me he could make me doubt myself. My coach, the person who was supposed to be my leader, my light, and guide during the fight, paid no attention to me and remained silent throughout my match. Even though I was young, I felt a strange mixture of emotions at that moment. I still had a deep hope that my Master would see me win and be happy for me; I was still holding on so tightly to the last light of hope that he might be an authentic coach, for once. I won the competition, but something deep inside me was slowly dying. I wanted to love and respect my Master, to see in him the image of the ancient masters, but that image was fading day by day, with his dismissive behavior toward us. I felt my soul trying to breathe new life into me.

Getting into the ring for my second fight was easy. So many things changed in my mind, things that made me eager to win over and over. I was hungry for victory. I wanted to break the shackles that had hampered me for so long, I felt like someone was fighting by my side in the ring. I was happy, motivated, energetic, and felt confident in my performance.

I won my second fight, followed by my third, fourth, and fifth fights. I felt like I had been born again. It was as if I had become a new person, with a new spirit, and a new outlook on life. I could not see my mother during my fights, as she seemed to have disappeared. However, there she was with my dad and Sally, standing by the rails surrounding the ring, cheering me on. At the same time, some of my teammates started to inch closer toward the ring, their faces filled with confusion over how I had won. It's as if they were seeing me for the first time. In truth, I was seeing myself for the first time too. I started questioning myself: "*Who was I?*" "*What happened to me?*" As the various questions swirled around in my head, my eyes carefully looked at my Master. He was still sitting in silence, smiling at the other coaches as they passed by, even as his face changed color.

My last match was about to start, and it was the final fight of the entire competition. All the coaches and athletes were standing and watching my fight as if God had planned this ending. At that moment, I saw my mother sitting on one of the upper benches in the arena close to my ring. She raised her hand to me and shouted loudly: "*God is with you.*" I smiled and looked up and said, "*Thank God.*" That moment was *my* moment. The moment I would show myself that I could win. This was the time to find out if I really wanted to win for myself. If I really believed in my capabilities.

After winning all my matches (6) and overcoming my fears, I joined Sally to be a Team AAU/USA member — We both won first place at the national level and got our spot on the national team

I entered the ring like never before, with a confidence in myself and deep trust in my abilities. My last fight was the best fight I ever had. I got a gap (by 20 points) in the final and won the Nationals. I won, not for my Master, but for myself. I proved that everything said about Sally and me was wrong. The stereotypes my fellow teammates and my Master held of me were wrong. I had defeated their lies, bullying, and harassment — and as a result, I became a member of the national team. This was the dream of every athlete in our sport. I joined Sally and spread my wings. Together, we both soared and became the athletes we had longed to be.

*I have become a member of the national team.
A dream of every athlete in our sport, I joined Sally and spread my wings—
Together, we flew and became the athletes we had longed to be*

At the close of the competition, many of the masters and coaches came to me and congratulated me and my Master. Our Master congratulated both Sally and me and left the competition immediately after my final match. I didn't get a chance to look him straight in the eye and tell him that the legacy of my sport taught me how to fight my battle with confidence and how to beat my opponent with respect —not him. The noble legacy of my sport had taught me all the things he had failed to teach me.

That day, our lives changed. We both found our inner strength. We freed the power within us that would lead us to victory. Sally was right when she said, "*The tough challenges we go through in our lives shape our thoughts and behaviors and try to force us to give up what we believe in, but the choice is in our hands to decide whether to give up, or to never compromise.*" We did not succumb to abuse and negativity. We did not concede. We were empowered by our beliefs and the belief in our abilities. We were still on summer break at the time, but we yearned to go back to school to tell everyone that *we* (Sally and I) were the new national team members. How amazing it would be to see the facial expressions of our peers when we told them we made the national team.

AAU/USA National Taekwondo Gold Medals

Training with the national team was one of our biggest dreams. Meeting the national team coaches and training with the best athletes in the country was a big deal for us, but unfortunately, that excitement would soon be shattered by a painful reality

Things weren't quite the same between our Master and us after the national championship. It didn't take more than a few weeks for him to once again reveal his true self, the persona he hid behind the mask he tried to wear after Nationals.

On January 15, 2017, the AAU national team conducted the first national team training in our hometown. We weren't sure about going to training yet. After the national championship, things had gotten worse with our Master, and he left us no choice but to change the hours we spent in the dojo so as to avoid him. We continued to train at home together as we had before. Our living room and media room became our new dojo. Our parents had to move all the furniture and put it aside to give us the proper space we needed to do the basic kicks of our training. We used the physical space outside our home for practice as well. We drew a ladder with chalk on our driveway and used it for a quick workout. We ran daily in our neighborhood with our dad to keep our pace and to increase our breathing capacity, while our mom would drive along in the car and cheer us on. We practiced at home and tried to avoid contact with our Master. Finally, it was time to train together with the national team, as it was mandatory. It was then that conditions with our Master quickly changed.

We drew a ladder with chalk on our driveway and used it for a quick workout

We used the physical space outside our home for practice, as well

We continued to train at home together as we did before. Our living and media rooms became our new dojo. Our parents had to move all the furniture and put it aside to give us the proper space we needed to do the basic kicks of our training

Sally and I are training inside our home

We ran daily to keep our pace and to increase our breathing capacity

Track training and warm-up before running

National Team Training (Jonah)

Training with the national team was one of our biggest dreams. Meeting the national team coaches and training with the best athletes in the country was a big deal for us but, unfortunately, that excitement would soon be shattered by a painful reality.

The moment we entered the dojo hosting the national team training, we felt the silence before the storm. The dojo belonged to a well-known coach in our state who was one of our Master's best friends. It seemed that our Master did not waste any time spreading rumors about us, after realizing we made the decision to leave his dojo and train at home instead. Training with the national team had been our dream, but all the coaches treated us rudely. We were surrounded by eyes full of disrespect and disgust toward us. It was as if we had committed a heinous crime against humanity. We tried to avoid our Master, but he didn't pass up a single chance to humiliate us. He was the head coach of the national team, so his commands were sacred and everyone had to follow them— not out of respect, but out of fear. Our parents sat outside the training room, as were the parents of many other athletes, so they could not hear what was going on. But when I looked at my mom she could tell something was wrong. Our Master called me "Go-go baby," like a crying or whining baby, and he spoke disrespectfully about our mother to the other coaches. We were forced to fight children who were older than us, in an effort to shatter our dignity and crush our confidence. This was a day we wish we could erase from our memory. Sadly, no one can eliminate the pain, but we can try to forgive and forget.

I couldn't maintain my strength anymore. The pressure was bigger than me, and it wasn't just coming from our Master. Regrettably, some of the other coaches and their athletes took this opportunity to reveal their true feelings about us. In a moment of weakness, I ran to the restroom to hid my tears from our parents. Sally tried to follow me, but our parents stopped her wanting to know what was going on. They looked for me but I was still inside the bathroom, shedding painful tears, while attempting to collect what was left of my crippled dignity. After a while, I heard my father's voice calling me, so I left the restroom with my head down, still trying to hide my tears. My dad asked me to look at him, seeking to cheer me up, but the moment I raised my head, my eyes fell on my mom. Her face was pale as if she had just seen a ghost. It seems our Master had continued humiliating us inside the training room, yelling at us and calling us nicknames. He had extended his cruel act of telling lies about our mother to the other coaches, telling them how embarrassed he was that we were on his team and that our family was always looking for trouble. The biggest lie of all was about how our mother coached us and caused lots of negativity in the dojo. His intention was to make sure no one would accept us if we left his dojo, ruining our reputation, not only as athletes, but also as a family.

Our father asked us to go to the car and wait there because he wanted to put an end to the problem with our Master; a problem that should have ended a long time ago. After a while, our father returned to the car with a smile on his face. He turned to us with fierce confidence and said, *"Your Master will not cause you pain anymore. That chapter of your life with him is over, starting today."*

That was the last day we were at the mercy of our Master. We felt the breeze of freedom for the first time. On that day, we did not know that our Master had threatened our father and swore he would not let us get anywhere in the sport if we left him. This was a direct threat to us, this time from the Master.

The Nightmare Continues (Jonah)

We thought we left our Master for good and had guaranteed our freedom to participate in the sport we loved in a different dojo, with a different master who respected us and whom we could respect. We were excited to find a new Master to protect us, stand by us, and motivate us, whether we lose or win competitions, regardless of race or religion. But unfortunately, we were wrong.

After the national team training, our parents started calling numerous dojos in our city to find the best one to join. We were surprised that none of these dojos wanted to cooperate with us or accept us. We wondered why they rejected us as we were national team members and state champions with gold medals in both! The rejection was hard for us, but we did not give up and continued our search, even after we kept getting turned down. Meanwhile, we continued training at the track field of our neighborhood school. We went to nearby parks to work on sparring techniques and exercises. The weather was hard to deal with and I can still feel the chill of the coldest days we had to contend with when we were training outside during the winter, or when we often had to train in the rain.

We were training in the nearby parks to work on sparring techniques and exercises after we left our former master and had no place to train

We had just turned eleven, and we felt like something was missing from our childhood. Our lives began to look different from the lives of other children. School was not easy for us. We had to deal with bullying from our peers, especially after we won Nationals. They persisted in their rejection of us, and that rejection spread to other children who also saw us as easy targets to express their negativity. We experienced much verbal abuse—we were called losers and weak. We couldn't understand why they acted this way. We couldn't explain how much they harmed us, or how painful their rejection felt. As a result, we felt hopeless and just wanted to be alone.

Bullying at school increased by some of our peers who found our national success a threat to their popularity. How was it possible we become national and state champions while they were the "cool" and "athletic" kids? I faced severe bullying by the group of popular athletes at school. They prevented me from every opportunity to enjoy recess time or even walking comfortably through the school lobby. They even fought my mental health and brought their persecution into the cafeteria, where no one talked to me during lunch. Sally faced the same situation as me, but she was more reasoned. She dealt with the rejection forcefully by ignoring any harsh words she heard. I was more vulnerable than Sally to these acts of bullying. I could barely breath freely due to the cruel bullying and mistreatment of our former Master. I wasn't ready for yet another fight. Besides, I was sure I would lose, because I was standing alone against so many bullies. At that time, our mother was the only reassuring presence we had. She spent all her time with us, whether when we studied at home, during our practice times outside, or while we trained in our home garage. She would sit on the track floor and cheer us up, cultivating hope in us as we trained on our own. Her motivational talks were the medicine that calmed our fears. She tried to heal our souls by planting a positive perception of everything that was going on with us. She made excuses for the bullies in our school and told us to understand they were still young kids like us, still learning the rules of life, and their behaviors do not come from hatred of us, but from lack of discipline.

We were both practicing in the track and field near our neighborhood

Training together at the park

Our mother tried to protect us from developing dark and negative feelings toward our peers. She has always said that positivity can erase negativity, and negative emotions will burn the person who carries them before they burn others. Our mother used to give us positive pep talks every day. We protected ourselves with this positive energy that kept our spirits and minds healthy. We ignored all the toxic behaviors targeted at us by some of our peers. We continued to focus on training ourselves at our home garage and on our academic performance at school, in the hopes of finding a dojo that would accept us students.

After a period of time without success finding a new dojo, and with many questions filling our minds, we knew the threat our Master had given our father the day we left him was not merely a scare tactic that would vanish, but a real threat. Our Master had indeed ordered every dojo in our city and cities nearby in our state to not communicate with us— his coercion even extended to other states! It was a massive shock for both of us to see how anyone could so easily escalate their hateful behavior toward us, as quickly as our Master did. How could this man's negativity, abuse, bullying, and harassment continue to threaten our freedom to practice the sport we love freely, even when we were out of his supervision? What kind of leader was he? What kind of teacher was he? What kind of power did he have to control coaches and other schools? What kind of humanity did he have in his heart to stand against children and order other dojos to stop us from participating in our sport? What kind of masters would accept and agree to follow his lead and order? So many questions ran through our heads without success in finding a logical answer to any of them. Darkness returned to cover our path; desperate thoughts invaded our minds and silence filled our hearts.

We felt betrayed by many masters who were supposed to be role models for the many values and principles that Taekwondo emphasizes. Where was the respect and discipline they taught their students? Was this really our sport? Do these masters respect the belts they wear, or were they even aware of the invaluable message their belts carries? The sport we loved was built on courtesy, integrity, perseverance, self-control, and an indomitable spirit. Where were these principles? How could these coaches ignore their oath, based on the values they pledged to respect?

We continued training at the track field of our neighborhood school

It was a devastating time for our family. Our parents repeatedly tried to bring hope to our hearts, but we were loaded with painful feelings. Regardless of our situation, we continued our training outside, in the backyard; inside the little space in our garage when we wanted to shelter from the rain; on the track, and even in our high school parking lot. Regardless of the obstacles, we didn't stop our training. Moreover, we decided to take the high road with our peers at school and did our best to avoid any negative contact with them. Ignorance was our friend at that time. We needed to disregard the way they treated us, so we could have a peaceful mind at school. But we felt tired and hopeless.

A few months went by, and we still had nowhere to go. There was no dojo, or any team wanted us. It was as if a curse had hit us. The cold weather outside was harsh, and we couldn't train every day. Therefore, we decided to move our training indoors. This proved challenging. There were no team members, a slippery floor, and limited space at our home. We were able to stay on track to train with some basic kicks and strength exercises, but we couldn't expand our capabilities beyond that.

After a while, our parents realized the negative impact our current situation was having on us and tried to help us by suggesting we choose a different sport; an athletic activity in which we could participate safely and freely. This was a very frustrating moment for both of us. Although we had had many painful moments up to that point, we had not yet felt this level of despair, as this was the moment when our parents, the people who kept us motivated and cheered us on, hit a dead end.

We strongly disagreed with our parents' suggestion we abandon Taekwondo, and that day we felt like our hearts were on fire. It was not a fire of anger or hatred for what happened to us at the hands of our Master, rather, it was a flame rising again after the fall. It was the flash of not surrendering to our limitations; the spark that ignited our resistance and inflamed our passion to continue the struggle for our freedom.

CHAPTER FOUR
The Rejection (Jonah)

We saw rejection as a trigger to redirect our conduct back to the right path. With all the disappointments that rejection carries, there is always a positive spark and hope that accompanies it. Rejection is the key we used to turn the power within us outward and redirect our constructive forces toward the proper path to reach our desired goals. Rejection ended up being the catalyst that led us on a new journey into the unknown.

Rejection had been the story of our lives. It was the shadow that accompanied us in everything we did and everywhere we went. Rejection magnified our desire to rise up and fight for our existence, our identity, and our dream. Rejection was the sword that cut through our weakness at its roots, making the fears in our hearts and minds bleed to death. Rejection was a constant throughout our lifelong journey to discover who we really are. During this journey of continuous rejection, we came to know our invisible power—the power that had lived silently within us for so long. Rejection gave us the ability to see how strong and capable we really are.

After that day, when we decided to decline our parents' suggestion to switch to another sport, we were determined to continue practicing Taekwondo. Moreover, after that day we made a firm decision not to allow the threat of our former master invade our minds with fear and terror. We planned to continue our training on our own even if no master, coach, or dojo wanted to accept us as their students because they feared our former master and his connections as head coach of the national team.

We were proud to be rejected by so many of these masters who acted like sheep with regard to our former master. We saw their rejection as a sign from God to reveal our strength and carve our own path without the help or guidance from any of these masters and coaches.

We decided to build our own names and show each one of these coaches, including our former coach exactly what eleven-year-old kids are able to achieve. Finally, we realized we had no choice but to create our own dojo; a dojo where we could train and participate in our sport safely and happily.

In our home garage, we removed boxes and things we stored in the garage to make space for our dojo

The Garage Journey (Jonah)

In our garage, we saw a place that could provide a stress-free and safe environment for training. However, our garage was full of boxes, bikes, and many gardening tools. After our parents agreed to support us on this new journey. Together began our first step in that quest— a step we didn't choose, but were forced to take. So, we started cleaning up our garage, removing unnecessary tools, and putting the rest into bins to ensure maximum space for the mats we bought to assemble a little ring we could use for sparring sessions.

Even with all the deep cleaning and organizing we did, we still ended up with limited space for our training. It seemed like an arduous undertaking and we felt we had to be strong if we really wanted to continue our uncharted voyage. We had to strengthen our minds and empower ourselves. To go down this path, we needed to arm ourselves with patience and passion. Patience was the key to our success.

Our home garage, where we cleaned and removed unnecessary items to make room for us to train

We both are practicing basic kicks at our new dojo, our home garage

We were training on our driveway, when the weather allowed us to work outside the garage

Garage Training, where we made a little space for our training — We both do kicks with paddles

We are working on developing our kicks in the garage

We are practicing our Taekwondo moves in our garage

I put up the mats we bought to make a training ring so we can do our kicks without fear of getting hurt if we fall

We finished building the dojo by ourselves in our garage

Our first official training in our home garage, the new dojo

Sally and I are working on our flexibility

Sally is working on her flexibility and performing an ax kick

We realized we were entering a new chapter of our lives. Although this new chapter might be rough, full of ups and downs, it would be unique — as we were the only ones who would take the lead and responsibility for filling the blank pages of our story with accomplishments. So, we will write our story without anyone's help, and it will be an honorable one.

Positivity was the energy we channeled to direct our minds and light up our hearts. Through positivity, we learned how to use the limitations our previous master brought us and tried to turn that criticism into motivational tools instead. Positivity fueled our passion for exploring our potential. Our passion grew faster and stronger every day.

We started our garage training while preparing for two big upcoming tournaments, the State Championships and the U.S. Open (a major international Taekwondo competition). It was an uncertain time for us, especially since we didn't have any coach helping us. At that point, a significant changed happened: one of the famous coaches in our state made a decision that caused him a lot of trouble later (this coach agreed to train us in secret). We were thunderstruck that he didn't want to let anyone know about his training with us. He kept telling us to be patient as he needed time to sort things out with our former master before he announced his readiness to allow us to join his team. It was really frustrating to hear those words of weakness from a Master who teaches martial arts to kids; who has a dojo and several athletes bowing down to show him respect. Sadly, our anticipation of assistance from this coach was thwarted before it even started.

After a few weeks of going to the coach's dojo before office hours for a short training session with him, and after a long talk with him and our parents, he agreed to let us come to the official night practice and meet his team. This experience left a painful scar inside us and shook our faith in our sport, which was supposed to provide us with confidence, self-esteem, and courage.

Our new coach decided to e-mail our former master to tell him he planned to let us join his team and sought our former master's permission before we could officially sign up. Unfortunately, this message was the shot that awakened the dormant volcano within our former master. He immediately sent his answer to this coach with a critical threat filled with hate, verbal abuse, and disrespect. Things got scary after that, and the coach hesitated allowing us join his dojo.

The State Championship would soon take place, and we were emotionally upset; our minds were not clear. Fear grew in our hearts, and darkness blocked our path. In March, I still remember being in the holding area waiting to be called for my first fight during the State Championship. I felt lonely and cold, and the new coach avoided sitting next to me and barely spoke to me. He seemed afraid to be seen with me.

Our parents were not allowed to be in the holding area, and the only face that provided me with security, empathy, and sympathy was that of Sally who came to sit next to me. None of the coaches or masters in the waiting area who knew us tried to talk to us; their athletes looked at us with disgust; a disgust built based on the feelings and perceptions of our master's false stories about us and our parents. While we waited, our former master took a step toward the holding area. This is the first time we had seen him since the National Championship training, the day we told him we were leaving his dojo. He was walking with confidence as if he owned the place. He spotted us, looked us straight in the eye, and said words that still ring in my head: "you will still be losers as you were before." His words terrified us and made us feel as if the blood had stopped moving through our veins. It was a terrible and shocking remark for a child to hear from an adult, especially a coach who was as strong and powerful as he was. He threatened us, knowing full well how his words would affect us both. How could we, two children, be expected to endure this hatred and survive in this environment?

At that moment, we realized there was no point to continuing our fight against him. On that day, we decided to end our fear, pain, and confusion. On that day we decided to quit our sport.

After waiting for a few hours in the holding area, I was called to the ring to start my first match. Sally and I had worked hard to prepare ourselves for this tournament, spending hours in our garage, on the track, and training in the rain. I walked toward the ring with heavy steps; I couldn't think or understand how I would stand in the ring to fight. I entered the ring with a defeated soul. I just wanted this day to end. I started to hate my sport and wished I had a magic wand to change everything. But magic is not real and cannot erase the awful pain I felt at that moment.

I stood in the ring, ready to give up all the remaining love I still have for my sport. My opponent was the same kid I competed against at the National Championship; the same one I had beat by a wide margin of points. I entered the ring area carrying so much disappointment on my shoulders—the small shoulders of that child who had been experiencing verbal, mental, and emotional abuse. The new coach followed me slowly, and kept his distance from me. It looked like he wanted to send a clear message that he wasn't with me. I sat on the bench, waiting for the referee to call me. I looked around and saw my new coach sitting far away from me. Our former master had succeeded to block the way for us to continue our sport. Unfortunately, he was not mistaken when he threatened our father—he would make sure we got nowhere if we decided to leave his dojo.

I lost my first match that day to a kid I had previously beat by a wide margin. That day we felt like we had nothing to give anymore. We didn't want to fight anymore, and we didn't have any strength or passion to continue our sport, a sport that showed us a reality that was quite different from the one about which we had read so many honorable stories.

Our parents waited for us outside the convention center where the State Competition was held. Our mother hugged us warmly and whispered in our ears, "*You are my heroes. Medals never define heroes, but courage and perseverance make heroes, and both of you showed courage today. Be patient; your day will come.*"

Our mother's voice awakened something in us. She was always the butterfly that gave us hope and spread positivity around us. We believed in her determination and trusted her words. Ironically, on that day we had both won the state's Distinguished Education Award for receiving excellent grades in school. This award was given by the state head of Taekwondo and required specific qualifications. After we received our prizes, a woman stopped us and asked Sally what prizes we had just won. Sally respectfully responded to the woman that these awards were for academic success. The woman liked how we spoke to her and she asked about our parents. So, I ran outside the competition grounds to bring my parents to meet her. Apparently, this woman was a journalist who covered the State Competition and wanted to interview us and ask us about Taekwondo and our academic success.

(LEFT) I am holding the State Academic Award presented by the President of the State Taekwondo Federation for academic excellence after I lost my matches but still I held a positive attitude. **(RIGHT)** Sally with the State Academic Award presented by the President of the State Taekwondo Federation for Academic Excellence

Me, during the interview with Ironwood production

Sally and I during an interview with Ironwood Productions at the State Championships

Sally tears up after I started crying in pain when I was talking about my experience with bullies

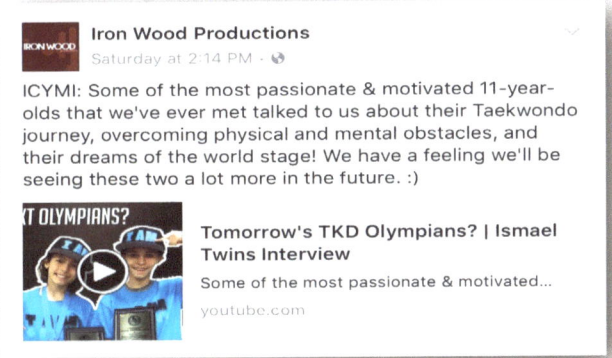

Ironwood production articles about our interview

We were featured on the World Taekwondo Federation website and FaceBook by the president of the World Taekwondo Federation after we shared our story on how we used our Taekwondo principles to achieve academic excellence

Our parents came and spoke with the journalist for a few minutes, and then gave her permission to speak with us about the prize. We had never done an interview before, so we couldn't predict what kind of questions would be asked. We both were cautiously excited about this interview. The journalist was very nice and she started asking questions about the award, eventually moving on to other topics regarding Taekwondo. She wanted to know about winning at the national level and what it was like being a team member. Unfortunately, these questions were the kind that brought us back to all the dark memories we had with our former master and how we could no longer enjoy being a part of the national team. We could not participate in any event with the national team, where the coaches took the team to a big competition, especially the trip to Spain.

Every question brought back all the painful memories; everything that had happened to us in the last two years, every struggle we'd been through, every difficult moment we had. We talked about how hard we trained, about losing weight, and about our experience with bullies. All the heart-wrenching memories played like a movie in front of me. I felt like the old scars of my pain had opened back up and, in a flash, these memories started flowing again—what had happened to me in the ring that day; how frightened I was of our former master; his cruel words to us in the holding area and his cold eyes that reflected the darkness in his heart.

At that moment, I felt a spark of pride light up as I realized how lucky we were. God's blessings were greater than any bullying behavior experienced at the hands of our former master or our peers. Although we had always felt close to God and had a strong belief in His abilities, on that day during the interview we felt just how close He was to us, protecting and guiding us. I could no longer hold back my tears, and in a moment of mixed feelings of honor, pride, and pain, I let my tears go. I let the pain go out, and I let the fear fade away. The interview made us see how small-minded our former master's behavior was and how it stemmed from insecurity and fear of our power. He and our peers were threatened by the power we had inside us.

During the interview, we could not say anything about our former master. No one would believe two children. Not one of the coaches who knew him, who abandoned us and treated us with awful disrespect would stand by our side. Talking about him would not change our situation, nor erase the pain he had caused. We could only beat our bullies by taking our sport to another level. To a level that no one had reached before, showing them the beauty behind our sport and the strength of two eleven-year-olds. In doing so, we would change the face of our sport. We would empower ourselves to overcome our obstacles, striving to achieve our goals no matter how many years it took and no matter how painful it was. We would prove to our peers that their negativity would never change the people we are. They would never again be able to break us.

Sadly, this new insight would not prevent future pain from coming our way. In fact, it was just the beginning.

My Story (Sally)

"We live one life, so live a life of meaning. Live a life you will be proud of, and always remember that God has given us a blank book, so choose wisely what kind of story you want to write in the book." These words of guidance were always central to our mother's advice to us. Everyone has a story to tell, and everyone has a journey to take. My story was one of failure and defeat, fear and doubt, love and freedom. At only eight years old I had already suffered injustice and cruelty.

My Taekwondo story was different than my brother, Jonah's, but it ultimately led to us discover we had the same goal and mission. I come from a gymnastics background. I was a competitive gymnast for about three years and, like many gymnasts my age at the time, I dreamed of being famous. I worked extremely hard, training for two to three hours daily after school. Our mother would drop me off at the gym and would then take Jonah to his Taekwondo training in a dojo across the street. Jonah played several sports, in addition to Taekwondo, but it didn't take long for him to realize that Taekwondo was his true passion. I was a bit fickle early on in my athletic career. The bars were my worst section of competition, but I worked really hard at every match. My teammates were the same girls from my elementary school; the same girls who teamed up the with boys to bully both me and Jonah. These kids always called me "fat" and told me that everything I wore made me look fatter.

Our mother was always motivating, encouraging, and supporting us. We talked to her freely about everything—the good and the bad. Our relationship with her was based on friendship, honesty, and respect. She never treated us like little children, and always gave us the opportunity to express our opinions on every subject, candidly and without fear.

My life changed one day, and I still remember how painful that day was for me. Still, most importantly, I also remember the birth of a strong and committed attitude toward the obstacles and limitations that had accompanied me thus far. At the time, I wasn't mentally strong enough to engage in a battle against negativity. I wasn't armed yet with the skills that would allow me to win my battle. I wasn't ready to fight for my identity and faith. Nevertheless, I showed a high level of courage and strength—greater than the ability of most eight-year-old children.

It was a normal competition day. I always loved my competition days. I loved dressing up in my competition leotard and doing my hair. This was the perfect day to show off all my hard work. As the competition was about to begin, all my teammates gathered around our coach for our final pep talk. I was so excited to start competing until the moment I discovered that my first station would be on the bars. My coach called my name to step in and start my routine. My heart was pounding hard and I felt like I couldn't breathe. I felt like everything around me was silent, waiting for me to start. I took my first step onto the mat, and in a desperate attempt to hide my fear, I stood firmly before the judges. I bowed to the judges, took a deep breath, and made my first jump. I raised my hand toward the crossbar and caught it strongly as if I was catching a star. I held tight to that bar with my small, soft hands. I performed my routine perfectly until the moment my hands slipped and I fell hard on my back. The most excruciating thing at that moment wasn't the shame or the physical pain I felt in my back, but rather the sounds of my teammates' laughter. They were making fun of me. Their laughter was like a knife stabbing into my heart.

My coach helped me stand up, I bowed to the judges and waited for my score; while my heart felt like it was bleeding, and my mind was choking from my teammates' laughter. I finally got my score and it was very low. However, I handled the situation with bravery, while whispering to myself that I still had three stations to go and I could raise my overall score if I did better on the next station. I was about to move onto my second station, but was stopped by one of my five teammates, someone who I also went to school with. She looked me in the eye and, in a hateful voice, told me I was the worst gymnast she had ever seen, and I should quit immediately. Her words crushed my dreams. I wished I could disappear, and I felt my dream vanish.

I immediately looked at the crowd trying to find my mother. I needed her love and warmth to melt the ice I felt in my heart. The moment my eyes fell on my mother, I was calmed by her smile and my mind lit up. My heart hugged her warm eyes. It was the silent force that I needed to strengthen my will to go on with the day. I remembered how I finished my three stations that day with the highest score for the entire season and perfected my routine. That day I knew I couldn't keep competing surrounded by negative people. I liked the coaches, my gym, and almost the entire team—but these girls were part of the team too and I couldn't face them after today. I believed in positive power and energy so I decided to turn my back on negative forces and look for a new path that would be surrounded by positivity. That day was my last day at the gym. I moved to another gym the following week and started a new class.

The coaches were so great and so supportive at the new gym and so were my new teammates. I worked hard between my gymnastics training and the evening classes at the dojo. I learned a very important lesson from my recent traumatic experience. I learned that when everything around us turns black, we need to keep our hearts white, our minds bright, and our eyes shining with hope. We need to thrive even in the darkest places. I did not let this traumatic experience stir up negative emotions in me. I learned that failure does not necessarily mean the end; failure sometimes means the beginning of a new, bright chapter, a fresh new beginning, and a new journey. Failure can open up new opportunities we couldn't see before. I have learned that I must not succumb to negativity or out-of-control forces if I want to succeed.

We have the power within us to create, dream, accomplish, heal, thrive, inspire, and overcome our limitations and obstacles. Through positivity, I learned how to expand my strength. I realized at the time that the difficult challenges we go through in our lives may shape our thoughts and behaviors and could even try to force us to let go of what we have, but the choice is in our hands not to give up and not to accept defeat.

My experience at the competition affected my performance abilities. Although my new team was very supportive, I couldn't forget how humiliated I was. It didn't take me more than two months to realize that my journey with gymnastics had reached its final chapter. I decided to leave gymnastics with honor and pride. I didn't give up, but I needed to try to avoid the negative forces playing into my head in an effort to kill all my remaining passion and desire for success. My new team was perfect in every aspect, but I needed a different path; I needed to know who I was and determine my goal in life.

My last gymnastic competition was held at Disney ESPN worldwide. In that competition, I achieved and conquered my fears. I won my station and perfected my bar routine without any mistakes. It was the best ending to a chapter of my life. However, I had to finish it to start a fresh new chapter, one that still lives on in my heart and I'm still excited about.

I joined Jonah in the dojo to be a full-time student of Taekwondo—that was the only requirement of my former Master for joining the competition team. He wanted me to have a complete commitment to training at the dojo. He didn't like the idea that I did gymnastics along with Taekwondo and insisted I had to choose one. Although I loved gymnastics very much, I realized that what my teammates did to me, how they treated me in the meet after I fell off the bars, was still in my head and I could not forget their laughter. I could not regain my competitive spirit, and the move to Taekwondo was a great step to work on my weight. I saw how Taekwondo could change my diet and my health.

My Taekwondo Journey (Sally)

Taekwondo was different from gymnastics. While gymnastics was about building and strengthening muscles, Taekwondo was about staying in shape. In Taekwondo, we must keep our weight in the right weight division, otherwise we would have to join a division with older kids who would kick harder and would be more difficult to beat. My goal after I joined Jonah was to have a reason to motivate me to work on my weight, especially after what I went through with the girls bullying in the gym and at school.

I was gaining weight rapidly due to thyroid hormone issues and working on my weight was my main goal now. I decided to lose weight for two reasons:

(1) my health and (2) to succeed in Taekwondo. I didn't want to leave any opportunity for these girls to call me a loser and fat again. I felt I needed to change their perception of me. At the time, I was more focused on how others saw me rather than how I saw myself. It hindered the way others saw me and lowered my self-esteem, but things started to change the moment I started seeing myself differently.

When I started Taekwondo training with Jonah, in the beginning, it was scary for me to fight—especially the boys—but Jonah encouraged me a lot. Day by day, I began to love Taekwondo through Jonah. I looked at him and could feel his love, passion, and happiness with Taekwondo through his martial arts and dojo training courses. I also noticed how cruel our previous master was to him. He called him names and insulted him during the sessions, especially during team training. Our former master was instilling fear and hesitation in Jonah's heart and mind. Jonah accepted these cruel behaviors as normal because he believed that our former master wanted him to become stronger and better than he was. The bullies at the dojo continued to make life difficult for Jonah, and the situation got even worse when some of them found purpose in tormenting him, aiming to shake Jonah's confidence, especially after he continued to win his matches against them during sparring sessions. Jonah faced a lot of defiant behavior and unwarranted cruel treatment for several years. His love of Taekwondo was the candle that lit the darkest days of the dojo. I've never seen anyone increase their love for something that caused them pain, as Jonah had with Taekwondo. The more he suffered, the more Jonah loved the sport. He saw something in Taekwondo that most did not. He cherished the principles and loved the history behind the sport. He relished the story of Taekwondo's warriors over the years and drew in the sweat of these legendary warriors who brought honor to the sport through their accomplishments. I tried to get Jonah to talk to our parents about what was happening to him and how he felt, but he was scared; he feared losing the sport he loved. He was afraid to confront our master, and I was afraid that I would be called a failure by some of our classmates. I couldn't stand seeing Jonah being humiliated daily and bullied nonstop, so I told our parents everything.

Things looked better after our parents confronted our master who admitted his behavior, but gave an unrealistic explanation to excuse it. He claimed that his method taught us discipline, which is the only way we would improve. Unfortunately, our situation didn't improve, and our master became tougher than ever. Throughout, my focus was on my goals, while Jonah did not give up any chance to train, even on weekends. He trained inside our house, running in the neighborhood, or going to the high school track. I started joining Jonah, and the more time I spent training with him, the more I started to love Taekwondo. Training with Jonah gave me a different view of Taekwondo. His enthusiasm and passion gave a different meaning to the sport.

It didn't take long for our former master to become more abusive and aggressive in his treatment of us with his verbal and mental abuse. We were training under fear, afraid of making mistakes, and anxious of being kicked by others while we practiced sparring. Our master created a very tense environment among his students. Our teammates adapted to his negative behavior, which created a very stressful training environment. The situation became worse when groups began to form within the team. Our master began encouraging team members to offend each other indirectly by asking them to hit each other's chest with their fists — without wearing protective chest guards. The sparring sessions had become a battleground that showed no mercy. Local competitions became a nightmare for both of us. We knew what we would face if we lost and what threat we would hear from him before entering the ring. I hated every minute of practice at the dojo, but loved my time training with Jonah at home. Jonah is a peaceful kid who always looks at others positively. He continually made excuses for their negativity toward him, and he always forgave anyone who caused him pain. His soul is pure and full of positivity and hope. He had a unique calm that made him absorb all the negativity around him and turn it into positive energy and motivation. Jonah's pure positive spirit surrounded me with peace, love, and serenity.

The setting became increasingly uncomfortable at the dojo, and the competitive yet passive dynamic in the team became an unhealthy environment in which to train. Our parents had to step in and talk to the master about the situation at the dojo, but he did not like their intervention and accused our parents of taking over our training. So, our father decided to speak to our master and politely ask for his permission to let us move to another gym. Our master felt the heat of the fire and asked our father to give him another chance. He alleged he would try to work to fix the situation in dojo, especially in the lead up to the national championship, which were around the corner. The master seemed serious about his promise, and so our parents believed him and we agreed to give him one last chance.

Preparations for the National Championship were very stressful. The team was divided, and our former master was ignoring us during training. It was hard on us to continue like that, but our mother's encouragement kept us going. While other kids' parents dropped their kids off at the dojo for training and then left, our mother stayed the whole time, sitting and watching us. It was the only way to stop the coach from tormenting us, and it was the best way to block his abuse until we finished the National Championship, and would be able to leave him permanently. Unfortunately, our Master began a more painful form of abuse. He began to ignore us completely, leaving us with no guidance during training. We had to watch the senior athletes to try and figure out what drills to do so we could train ourselves.

Jonah and I trained together all the time, because no one wanted to partner with us. Team members complained that we kicked too hard and so they refused to spar with us. The national training came to an end and we were more mentally prepared than physically and ready to start our battles. It wasn't a competition to earn a spot in the national team anymore; it was a competition to win the battle of rejection, bullying, and mental abuse that was targeting our minds in the dojo and in our elementary school at the hands of some of our peers. We were more than ready to start our fights, and we were determined to win.

We traveled to Nationals with hearts full of hope and determination. Jonah and I had different reasons for becoming national team members and winning Nationals. Jonah was working on his goal of winning Nationals and making the national team so that he could end the suffering and prove to our Master, the team, and the kids who were bullying him at school that he was not a loser. I had a different goal in mind: I wanted to win and end this nightmare. I wanted to leave the dojo. I wanted my freedom back, and I wanted to be who I really was.

We fought at the National Championship with complete focus on our goals, and we won. We were the only ones from the whole team who won and made the national team. Our team did not like the results, nor did our master. He started making indirect threats that if we left him, no one would accept us, and we would get nowhere. Our parents insisted on their decision to leave the dojo and several times asked our master to let us leave in peace. His ego did not allow himself to accept this. He started declaring war on us, and this time it was a direct attack.

During the national team training that was held in our city, our former master directly abused us mentally, verbally, and emotionally. He didn't miss a single opportunity to humiliate us and show us that he was in control of everything, and could do anything he wanted to us without objection from any of the coaches of the national team.

That day was the end of our story with our former master. Our father told him we couldn't stay with him and that he had decided to take us out of the dojo and look for another dojo and another master. Our master was very angry that day, and threatened our father that he would make sure we would not get anywhere without him; he would ensure that no coach would accept us in their dojo.

We thought our story with our former master was finally over that day, but we were wrong. It had just started. Our former master's threat wasn't just a string of unintended words uttered in a moment of anger, they expressed a decision he had made and had been preparing to say for a long time. Our chapter of pain continued. Although we were unduly punished, the isolation, impediments, and obstacles we regularly faced were no match for our faith and determination to achieve our goals.

CHAPTER FIVE
The Isolation (Sally)

*We continued our training in the garage and at the park —
In addition, we did physical activities on the track at our community high school*

The summer was hot, and training outside was very stressful for us as kids. Nevertheless, we continued our practicing as we had before. We trained in our home garage, ran daily in our neighborhood, and did some physical activities on the track at our community high school.

Events seemed to be happening slowly while we awaited answers from a couple of well-known coaches in our town and cities near us regarding they would accept us onto their teams. Meanwhile, we prepared for the State Championship, worked on our weights, and kept the daily workouts by ourselves.

Training outside, at our neighborhood high school Track field

Training outside, at the track field

Training outside at the track field, running, and doing some physical activities

Training outside at our community high school track field

Our training was at the track field, where we ran and did physical activities

Unfortunately, the bad news came to us as no shock. There were no coaches, dojos, or masters who wanted us to be part of their teams. Things seemed strange; we were members of the national team and state champions. We were known for our strength in sports. How could coaches not want us? So, we didn't give up and called one of the coaches we felt comfortable around.

We thought we could train with him until things were settled between him and our former master, but it didn't happen. Our former master admonished him and succeeded in intimidating the new coach by threatening him. The new coach showed fear and weakness and was always reluctant to be around us in public, especially during the State Championships. This continual rejection took a toll on us mentally, as did the traumatic bullying experience we endured in the holding area during the State Championships from our former master. No coach had the courage to stand by our side. How could they choose to stand by us and instead stand by the national team's head coach, one of the country's strongest coaches? From the start, it was a losing battle for us. We finally had to realize that our former master's strength and power could not be defeated by just two kids.

The only positive developments that happened to us in the State Tournament was the academic excellence award we got from the President of the State Taekwondo Federation, and our interview with an online Taekwondo Channel that wanted to ask us questions about the award we received. In that interview, Jonah couldn't hold back his tears, nor could I, when he started talking about bullies at school. We were eager to talk about our former master, and about the team and coaches who dismissed us, but we promised our parents to turn this page of our lives, and leave behind all that abusive negativity. Either way, if we talked or didn't talk, no one would believe us, and we wouldn't receive any comfort. Our mother wanted us to heal through embracing positive thoughts. If we continued talking about the pain, we would never feel the healing that could touch our hearts and minds.

The two events that both happened to us at the State Championships—receiving the academic award and giving the interview—changed the way we thought about the obstacles we faced in the past and those we will face in the future. That was the moment when we realized that even if we attacked our previous master in his domain with his strength, wielding power and connections, he wouldn't be able to beat us in our domain. God created us with powerful minds and emotions, so why not channel those agonized feelings into becoming motivating forces? Why not use our brains and find ways to train, compete, and win, instead of letting our coach decide everything for us like before? What prevented us from creating our identity and carving our own path?

It took us several weeks to start getting back to normal and return to our daily training. Middle school was about to start, and we had to reevaluate everything. We had to be more realistic and know what was really important to us; we had to decide how and where to train.

We realized that life doesn't come with a road map or instructions; we must travel through life alone, striving to reach our chosen destinations. What ultimately makes someone strong is how they react to the twists and turns that life throws at them. It was clear to us that quitting our sport wasn't an option, and neither was transitioning to another sport. We kept rewatching our interview at the State Championship and it all clicked. We focused on our answers when the journalist asked how we were able to maintain such strength in our minds and how we could train effectively, in spite of the bullying. She then asked us, "What advice would you give to other children your age?" To which I answered, *"Don't let any struggles or obstacles stop you from what you have in mind; what you want to do later in life, or defining your goal. Stand firm through the hard times, and you will get to the good times."* Jonah then added, *"Face your fears and don't give up. Keep trying. Practice diligently and you will achieve your goals."*

At this point, fall was fast-approaching. School had already started, and we had to find somewhere indoors to practice before the weather got any colder. We couldn't keep training outside all of the time, and we needed more professional equipment for training. We asked our parents if we could turn our garage into a gym.

After much discussion with our parents, we convinced them to let us have a gym in the home garage. So, we started the process of building a dojo at home. It took us a while to prepare the dojo. Even though it was small, with tools packed off to the side, we were glad to finally be able to kick and train again. Our parents gave us all the money we had saved so we could buy basic mats and equipment to start our sparring sessions together.

The initial year of our first formal training in the garage was a torturous experience for both of us. We had trained in the garage before, as well as in the garden, on the track, and indoors for two years. However, this time it was completely different. The picture was crystal clear now. Training in the garage was the only option left to us. We had nowhere else to go. All the "good" masters did not want us in their dojos.

So, we sat down and talked about our plans, our goals going forward. We knew this year would be different from the last two years. We were completely alone now — with no coach, no master, no dojo, and no teammates. It was just the two of us in a small garage, with just a mat, and a dream to fulfill.

The garage was isolating, but nevertheless, we decided we had to embrace the struggles, challenge ourselves, and strive to advance our capabilities. To become stronger, we had to focus more deeply on what is most important. We knew we had no choice but to live our journey with passion and to keep our souls vigorous. We must strengthen our faith in our abilities and in the power God has bestowed upon us.

Our garage training was not as much physical as it was mental training. In every struggle we faced, and with every limitation we encountered, we built a mental defense mechanism. We were building our minds to be strong, and we were opening our vision to new options. We knew that together, we could progress forward, break the chains that had bound us before, and live a life of passion. We focused on enriching our minds by increasing the intensity of our training. There is no better challenge to the mind than intensifying the level of difficulties placed on it. We choose more advanced-level drills and employed more professional techniques. We read many books about the power of perception and how we could manipulate our minds to be powerful. We read a lot and applied what we learned to our training. Education was the only weapon we could use to fight our battle against the injustice, rejection, racism, and humiliation that had befallen us.

CHAPTER SIX
The Suffering (Sally)

There will always be obstacles, adversity, challenges, doubters, and setbacks along the way of achieving a person's life quest. Although we struggled to face all these difficulties, without having to cope with and overcome suffering and pain, we would never become stronger and smarter than before. We have a power within us that keeps whispering to us, telling us to keep moving forward, to keep trying, to keep believing in our abilities, and to maintain our trust in the process. Garage training tells the story of our struggle and defeat. The obstacles we faced caused pain, controlled our minds, and drained our emotions. They obstructed our dreams and spread darkness around us. But we can overcome our obstacles by making the journey unforgettable and endeavoring to fill our travels with happy moments. So let the sun rise, let the darkness fade away. We believe that within each of us there is a powerful force that makes us heal and smile again.

Our former master's arrogance was greater than we expected. He could not accept the fact we had not yet broken from his constant bullying. He felt he had not yet seen us suffer enough, when he decided to shut all the doors in our faces. He had not yet satisfied his vigorous appetite to offend us. He had not quenched his inner thirst to make our hearts suffer again and trample our souls. He, unfortunately, wanted more. His hunger to destroy us increased, so much so, that we felt like the grim reaper was chasing after us. He followed us every place we went and every event we attended. His hypercritical and abusive behavior haunted us. He was like a ravenous wolf, with its sharp fangs and nails, waiting for its prey.

The depth and breadth of our former master's malicious reach began to become clear to us shortly after we accepted a strange invitation from a well-known coach. This coach sent a message to our mother on social media inviting us to a large training camp hosting national team players from a foreign country. In his invitation, the coach added that "we would fit right into their level of training." We were pure, innocent kids, who still believed in and still respected these masters of our sport. So, we bought airline tickets, booked our hotel rooms, and headed to Florida where the boot camp was being held.

The moment we got to the main dojo we realized why we had been invited to that camp. The coach hosting the camp humiliated and mistreated us. He claimed to the guest coach from the foreign country that our mother trained and coached us; that she told us what to do and what not to do, and decided who we train with.

Jonah lined up with young children to train with them; despite the fact they were not in his age category or in the weight division. Jonah politely appealed to the coach to move him into the right division, like other athletes his age. The coach did not like what he viewed as an arrogant request. As he yelled in Jonah's face, the coach told Jonah that our mother must have told him to ask that question. The coach then insulted us both emotionally and mentally. After camp ended, the coach held a swimming party and invited all the athletes who participated in the camp, except for us. He refused to allow us to be a part of the end of the camp celebration. It was the most painful and mortifying feeling we have ever experienced. We were 11 years old and had just come out of a very painful bullying experience with our former master. We weren't ready to go through another excruciating encounter. This coach was one of our former master's best friends and, distressingly, he planned for all of these agonizing incidents to happen.

The worst thing about this new master's actions toward us was that he forgot he was the leader, and that the athletes from his team were watching and learning from him. His abusive behavior was adopted by some of the athletes who unfortunately did not pass up any opportunity to show their negative feelings toward us. Kids learn from adults. Kids are not born knowing to bully; rather, they learn bullying by watching others. We, too, learned from adults, but because we grew up with two wonderful parents who emphasized the importance of principles, respect, values, and morals, we copied those traits for ourselves. It was extremely frustrating and sad to witness the negative, destructive behavior of this coach rubbing off on his athletes.

In Sorrow, There is Strength! (Sally)

The three of us cried a lot that day, me, Jonah, and our mom. It was a shocking moment for us. We had so many questions running through our minds, without finding a single answer to any of them. We were confused and wondered how this man could be a coach. How was he proficient in a sport built on respect;

one that calls for discipline? On that day, we realized that our former master's pursuit to ambush to assault our souls had just begun — and that what we had experienced before was just a drop in the bucket of what he had in store.

Our determination to continue our journey together in the garage, in spite of all the limitations, obstacles, pain, and embarrassment we had faced thus far came from our zealous allegiance to the positive vision and attitude we both swore an oath to adopt. We learned how to deal with pain by employing a positive outlook on everything that happened to us. We had to learn to deal with pain and disappointment. Through the process, healing came to our broken hearts and minds.

Dealing with pain and obstacles taught us that no matter what comes our way, we would not respond with negativity. We would never counter hate with hate. We would never allow negative forces control our belief in ourselves, our principles, and our faith in God. We would resist the darkness with discipline. We would fight back with respect. We would fight with a positive attitude because we respect ourselves and respect our sport.

Through the obstacles we encountered, we learned to push ourselves outside our comfort zones. We would continue to enrich our minds with knowledge. We read a lot of books about the human body—its mind, muscles, nerves, etc.—We also read many articles on rejection. Through education, we found refuge from the abuse of our former Master. We learned how to discover new abilities within us. However, undoubtedly, the most important thing we learned by facing the obstacles we encountered is how to dig deep within us and find our deepest strength. Through our extensive research and reading, we became aware of the mind–body connection and how powerful our minds become through education.

Encountering obstacles can teach us who we really are. Our obstacles can show us a new version of ourselves, one that is undefeated and unbreakable. The more emotionally and mentally we are affected by abusive behaviors or bullies, the stronger we become mentally, as well as, more positively motivated. The realization we are stronger than we thought was becoming clear to us. Rejection was both our enemy and our motivation. Although we didn't know the secret behind this unreasonable rejection, our former master's motives became clearer to us later, during our years of isolation in the garage. We believed in God and trusted Him. He was our deepest strength. Rejection motivated us to trust God more and look for additional ways to improve.

Our Trust in God (Jonah)

We understood that motivation was the only fuel that would allow us to achieve our goals. Like many people, we always kept looking for motivation from others. We thought that attending this coach's training camp would inspire us and fire up our enthusiasm. We felt that if we went back to training with other athletes and coaches, we would win our battle against our former master. Unfortunately, however, we didn't realize that we didn't need to win the fight, because the real battle hadn't even started.

We developed a new vision as a result of our traumatic experience during that boot camp. Through participation in the boot camp we both realized that we were constantly waiting for others to motivate us, while forgetting that we had the most powerful source of motivation within us. We didn't need to look outside to find our motivation; we just needed to push beyond our limits and obstacles to achieve our goals. We knew we have a strong inward impulse within us that causes us to act, and that is why humans are called the supreme creation of God. God created us and implanted in His creations powerful skills and abilities. We are all talented and we all have the potential to succeed, but we need to believe in ourselves. We must have confidence in our abilities and need a deep belief in our Creator, our God.

Our journey taught us that the more we stretch our awareness and challenge our limitations, the more resilient we become. We realized that if we wanted to survive and thrive, we needed to find the strength to expand our capabilities, limits, and patience. We must be flexible and adapt.

As our vision of our obstacles changed, we re-evaluated our goals and plans. We began striving to train not to *find* ourselves but to *create* ourselves. The power is ours. The journey is ours. The gift is ours. We are the only ones upon whom we can rely. We are the only ones who control our success.

To develop a strong mindset, we realized we had to continue to ward off obstacles and limitations. We had to challenge our minds to resist the force against us and empower the force within us. We needed to keep fighting; we couldn't give up and we couldn't keep turning our backs on our obstacles. If we did that, we would give up whenever we face an obstacle later in life.

We continued our garage training alone, while trying to balance the time spent there with the time spent at school and on our school work. At the same time, we developed a defense mechanism we used with the schoolmates who harassed us: we swore to always take the high road. We used this defense mechanism to avoid unnecessary fights with bullies as they entered middle school alongside us.

We hoped, dreamed, and imagined the path we wanted to follow. But unfortunately, many forces were stronger than us at that time. No matter how often we changed our minds with strength and our hearts with positivity, there were always many negative forces bigger than us, bringing us back to where we started.

Our journey taught us that the more we stretch our awareness and challenge our limitations, the more resilient we become. We realized that if we wanted to survive and thrive, we needed to be flexible with the struggles we encountered.

We needed to find the strength within us to expand our capabilities, our limits, and our patience. We must be flexible and adapt. We felt the need to recognize our impediments, learn more about our struggles, read more about the human mind's capabilities, and create a harmonious relationship with our limitations. This is how we would be able to lead ourselves, thus becoming our own masters. The garage had become our laboratory where we studied our opportunities and expanded our knowledge to fit those opportunities. We changed our training techniques to work more on strengthening our mindset instead of practicing regular Taekwondo training. We found our mindset shift to be a game-changer for the success we had in the garage.

The teachers at our middle school were wonderful. They surrounded us with positivity, support, and encouragement. Middle school provided us with We had the best three years any kid could dream of. We enjoyed the time we spent with our teachers, the school management, and the overall experience. Even though the same bullies continued harassing us, we can honestly say that middle school was our best learning experience so far.

We began striving to train not to *find* ourselves but to *create* ourselves.

Thanks to our changed mindset, nothing bothered us, and no one was able to make us nervous. In fact, we became more sympathetic to the kids around us, as we realized they were drowning in their own negativity, and burning themselves even before they succeeded in burning us. We built a strong positive shield around us and laser-focused our minds on our goals and program. We were determined to avoid any unnecessary distractions instigated by those bullies, whose lives were devoid of purpose, dreams, or plans — that is why they chose to fill the emotional and intellectual voids in their lives with negativity toward others.

Our disappointment with these children transformed into guilt. We felt we needed to help them release their negativity. We knew that their negative behavior and bullying was a mask they wore to hide a weakness or conflict within them. We decided that by ignoring how they treated us, eventually they would reach a point where they would give in, and then finally reduce their level of anger and hatred toward us and others. We were determined not to give them what they wanted, not to engage in the same behaviors— and we elected not even to tell the school administration about them.

We felt a need to help them diminish their acts of bullying by reducing any unnecessary negative interaction with them. We believed that our positivity, we could overwhelm the negativity within them and hopefully help heal their hearts. Remarkably, our mission was a success, and the acts of bullying against us by some of our peers slowly declined. We looked at life in a very unique color. We believe that colors and shades bring vitality to our lives. Colors and their hues add meaning and provide motivating direction to our lives. Colors lead us to our purpose in life. So, we thoughtfully chose the colors we wanted to add to our lives and the colors we wished to see in our lives ahead.

We hoped, dreamed, and imagined the path we wanted to follow in life. But unfortunately, many forces were stronger than us at that time. No matter how often we fortified our minds with strength and filled our hearts with positivity, there were always numerous negative forces bigger than us bringing us back to where we started.

During this time, we had been preparing to make the competition team that would represent our country and state, scheduled to take place in Canada. This was one of the biggest competitions in North America. It was not easy for us to train for this significant championship on our own in our garage; trying to figure out the exercises and moves that would help raise our level to that of the other athletes who were well known in our state and country — especially since it had been a year since we trained with a team or under the supervision of a professional coach. There had been a few times here and there where we joined other teams for a day or two through training camps we paid to be a part of, but that was it. Training together alone in the garage was very stressful for both of us.

As our vision of obstacles changed, we re-evaluated our goals and plans.
We began striving to train not to *find* ourselves but to *create* ourselves.

The power is ours. The journey is ours. The gift is ours. We are the only ones upon whom we can rely.
We are the only ones who control our success.

We needed to keep fighting; we couldn't give up,
and we couldn't keep turning our backs on our obstacles.

The garage had become our laboratory, where we studied our opportunities
and expanded our knowledge to fit these opportunities.

We changed our training techniques to work more on strengthening our mindset. Instead of doing regular Taekwondo training, we found our new mindset to be a game-changer for the success we had in the garage.

We built a powerful positive shield around us and focused our minds on our goals and program.

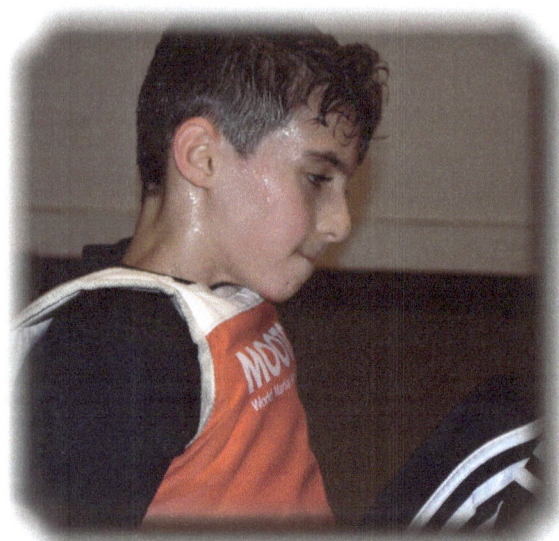

Training in the garage limited our creativity and threatened to stamp out our positivity and motivation. Still, we both knew we had to learn to achieve balance in the narrow, limited paths we walked along on our journey.

The Journey Toward Developing a Strong Mindset (Jonah)

Our garage was very small and crammed with tools and storage boxes. The dust covered cartons filled our lungs and made it hard to breathe. To make matters more difficult, we couldn't open the garage door—in the summertime, it was sweltering hot, and in wintertime it was extraordinarily cold. Training in the garage limited our creativity and threatened to stamp out our positivity and motivation, but we both knew we had to learn to achieve balance in the narrow, limited paths we walked along on our journey. We needed to know how to stay on the right track and not get caught up in the obstacles that burdened us. We had to learn to control our obstacles by controlling our steps.

We began to train our minds to see these obstacles as opportunities. We had to stop being afraid of the limitations around us. We needed to adapt to our obstacles, understand every angle, and merge with them to be one body and system. We must make our minds see our obstacles as allies, not enemies. We needed to overcome our fears, doubts, and hesitations at that moment, and strive to conquer our fears. We understood we had to trust our abilities and boost our confidence. In this way, we could train our minds and hearts to be patient, and not get frustrated with the limitations surrounding us.

We couldn't open the garage door—in the summertime, it was sweltering, and in winter, it was extraordinarily cold.

When confidence is found, we are able to overcome great obstacles, and turn our toughest challenges into our strongest victories.

With confidence, we could overcome great obstacles and turn our toughest challenges into our strongest victories. We must never stop trying until we can take control of ourselves and conquer the fears inside our minds. This was our hardest battle. This was a battle we had to win if we wanted to create our own path and identity.

We learned that our brain is a multifunctional entity that can think, plan, manage, and give orders to our nerves and muscles.

At that moment, we realized that Taekwondo was no longer the sport we participated in to win medals, or to be one of the athletes who would stand on the podium. Instead, Taekwondo had become our life's journey toward claiming our existence and forming our identities. Taekwondo had become a cause for action and the tool we used to stay motivated for excellence in every aspect of our lives—whether it was in school through our academic performance, in our community through volunteering opportunities, or through our goal of carving ourselves a path and proclaiming the kingdom within us. It was a kingdom we built on the foundation of our inner strength, positivity, and confidence.

Our journey was filled with curiosity. We have always had the impulse to keep moving forward. Curiosity leads to new paths, intensifies the power of self-learning. It can fuel the power within us to conquer, learn, and discover. Driven by our curiosity, we revealed our inner strength through a long and continuous examination of our minds. We learned that our brain is a multifunctional organism that can think, plan, manage, and give orders to our nerves and muscles. Our brain is the main operating system responsible for raising the level and intensity of our training by providing us with visual endurance, speed, reaction, and cognitive abilities.

Instead, Taekwondo had become our life's journey toward claiming our existence and forming our identities.

We faced a harsh reality—at that time we needed partners to test our abilities and capabilities. We realized that to awaken the strength within us, we had to step up the challenges. We needed to train with the others, but there was no chance of having a team in our city that would accept us. Even the coach who had agreed to have us before—though he was kind, gentle, had promised to let us join his team, and was ready to take on our former master—finally succumbed to the threats he had received from our former master before the State Championship. We were left with no choice but to search for a dojo outside our city to train in, and find new instructors, coaches over whom our former master had no power or authority.

We remembered that during the State Championships we met a new coach who had just arrived in the state and opened a new dojo, after retiring from coaching an Olympic team in a foreign country. At the time, this coach invited us to come to train with his new team—apparently not knowing our story and the difficulties we were having with our former master. We took his offer seriously and traveled to the nearby city for a training camp he was hosting. This was an opportunity to prepare and check our sparring abilities against other partners. After more than four hours of driving, we arrived at the dojo. We were warmly welcomed at the camp, which was very motivational. Furthermore, the feeling of having a normal training session in a real dojo, like many other athletes, was worth the long drive. We spent two days training, testing our abilities, and were ready to earn our place on the state team for the state qualification competitions. Before we even got home, the coach expressed his admiration for both of us and asked if we would join his team. We were so excited to feel accepted by this coach and we thought that we had finally arrived at a peaceful place to develop and excel. Sadly, we were wrong, as we had been many times before.

We excitedly accepted his offer and joined the team. On Friday nights, every other weekend, we drove to train for one hour at the dojo. Our father was traveling a lot at that time for his work. Nevertheless, he would come home on Friday after a hard, busy work week and drive us the four hours to practice, so we could get under an hour of training with the team, only to go home Saturday morning. This arrangement caused a lot of uncomfortable situations for us, as we didn't feel like we belonged to the team. We didn't learn anything because the team didn't train on Saturdays, which left us only a short fighting session with the team on Friday nights. These Friday-night sessions weren't challenging for us, since the team had just formed and the athletes were mid-level players who had only participated in the local tournaments.

We had paid money to join the team, but unfortunately did not receive what we had been promised. We started avoiding going to train at the new dojo, but continued our monthly tuition fees. We looked at this money as a gift to say "thank you" to this coach for opening up his gym for us. However, we discovered later that this kindness we were repaying had never been his intention at all.

The Battle has Begun (Sally)

State qualification arrived, and we were ready to follow through with our plans to win this competition and move on. However, our plans were different from the plans of the state coaches. All the coaches and teams that attended the qualifiers somehow led back to our former master. It was so scary and exhausting. Fighting a battle we knew we might lose —not because of ourselves, but because of other people's stereotypes of us.

We felt as if darkness was all around us that day. It was scary and bitter. This darkness had the power to shake our confidence and shatter our strength, but we were dedicated to winning this battle. It was not our first battle with negativity and obstacles, nor was it our first experience battling our former master's shadow; the shadow which kept chasing us. If we were going to win we needed to reflect the positive power within us to lighten the surrounding darkness. We had to trust our abilities and never underestimate the power within us. We needed to unleash our inner strength. We had to win.

We didn't have a coach sitting in our chair that day, so we had to fight alone, just like we trained alone. However, we were happy to see some familiar faces there, like the coach whose team we joined. We got into the ring, and I had straight qualifications as no one in my division showed up that day. On the other hand, Jonah had to win three fights to claim his victory. Jonah was energetic, determined, and very focused on his goals. He struggled so much with our former master who had always insulted him during competitions, sent him into his fights with self-doubt, and constantly called him a "loser." Jonah's bad memories haunted him like a ghost whenever he entered the ring, causing him to always fight multiple battles simultaneously — one against his opponent and the other against his self-doubt.

We thought that Jonah had received his qualifications that day after winning his three fights. However, the case was not as simple as it was supposed to be. We were surprised that the Vice President of the State Taekwondo Federation back then wanted Jonah to fight two more fights with two kids who were heavier than him and weren't even in his age division. He said that if Jonah won over these two competitors, he would earn his qualifications and join the state team. Naturally, our parents were very angry with this treatment. Politics, discrimination, and corruption in sports were really unstoppable at the time. It was like a contagious virus that infected all the coaches and spread to the athletes as well.

Jonah insisted on accepting this challenge and began his battles. There was no electronic system for counting kicks, and the referees were allies of our former master and his best friends. Jonah had to kick so hard, so as to not give any of these referees a chance to question his skilled maneuvers. It was one of the most stressful days for our mother, who had wanted Jonah to refuse to participate in this unfair fight. Jonah was very strong and showed professionalism and talent that day. After two fierce battles, he defeated the boys, both of whom were in the weight division above him. He thought it was over at that moment, but it wasn't easy for our former master and his friends to accept that we both had qualified.

At the time, the Vice President of our State Taekwondo Federation raised the competition bar even further for Jonah and insisted that he fight another boy he aimed to add to the team. This behavior was very unprofessional and disrespectful to the sport, as the battle became more like a street fight and not a state qualification. But, we knew that the coaches, including the State Federation Vice President, were all like chessmen in a chess game and our former master was moving them around the way he wanted. Our former master's orders were for them not to let us win, so that we couldn't go too far without him. What a humiliation for the sport we honor. These were not the honorable principles of Taekwondo. He was disgracing the sport's integrity, respect, and discipline with his corrupted character.

We were in the devil's den by ourselves and faced negative forces stronger than us and our parents, but not stronger than God's will. On that day, God wanted Jonah to win. God showed him that positivity always wins, and that hard work always pays off. Jonah put all his strength into that final match. It was painful for me to see Jonah standing in the ring fighting the kid while the coaches cheered for Jonah's opponent, as they counted up points for the other kid and ignored Jonah's kicks.

To earn his points, Jonah realized he had to kick ruthlessly hard in the head, so hard that no one could question whether or not he deserved a point. Jonah perfected his talent, abilities, and sportsmanship that day, earning his place with respect. That day, he was reborn. He came out of all the fights he fought with a new mindset and psyche. However, he held on to the one character trait that drove him to win: his positivity. Jonah trounced his weakness that day, and this victory empowered him.

Negativity Aggravates the Positivity Within Us

Jonah refused to let the obstacles he faced or his limitations determine his strength that day. Instead, his fortitude crushed his limits, unleashing his inner strength.

That day, we realized that mastering our concentration would require strong willpower. Extreme willpower would enable us to intentionally ignore distractions while staying focused on the task at hand. Jonah took notice of every plan against him. He knew that to win he had to clear his mind to focus on channeling and redirecting all of the negative feelings that were reflected toward him. He had to use that negativity and turn it into positive motivation. Through his struggles, he saw an opportunity to make his way without any help from anyone.

There are two different types of accomplishments in life. The first is what comes from the strength within us due to our endless efforts. The second is the achievement that comes thanks to the help of others who paved the way for us. Although both are called accomplishments, with time only the original achievements remain the real ones—meaning, those that we achieved without the help or approval of others.

Jonah wisely decided the person he wanted to be that day. He chose to stand firm in the face of the storm and fight his battles alone. Jonah chose to earn his reward with his efforts. It stopped being a qualifying tournament for him when the coaches changed the rules of the game and stopped respecting our sport's principles. They transformed the competition into a battle of dignity and identity. The significance of that day awakened our minds. We had to complete what we started, and we needed to finish the match against these individual strengths. These coaches showed us their desire to restrict our success and shake our confidence. They wanted to emphasize that what our former master had told our parents before was not merely words of intimidation uttered in a moment of anger, but rather a cruel and decisive threat to prevent us from practicing our sport. They were playing a dirty game to pressure us to quit.

Despite winning our battle—against the odds—what deeply disappointed us that day was our recognition that the implicit honor and respect we had for these influential figures in our sport were gone forever. Our perception and vision of our sport had become blurry. The most important lesson we learned from that painful experience was that God's abilities are greater and more powerful than those coaches. Faith and trust in God are the two positive weapons we have used against negative forces since that day.

We both understood that if we wanted to become stronger and more powerful, we needed to suffer, as that is how we would develop resilience. We realized that the pain and disappointment we faced that day gave us another perspective on our purpose. It changed our vision and shaped a new meaning of our sport for us. We had to make our decisions judiciously and see what was most important to us. We needed to avoid getting into useless fights; give up fighting negativity—but at the same time, we were entering into the fight of our lives. We needed to foster positivity within ourselves and direct our focus to one goal: winning the battle against our limitations. We had to prove that the prison our former master decided to put us in would be the incubator where we would develop a deep vision and grow strong wings so we could fly over all the walls surrounding us in our garage.

Education is Power

After that day, we started our preparations for the Canada Open, an international competition we were eager to attend. We trained hard in our garage while maintaining a high level of focus on our academic excellence at school. We felt that both things complemented each other—our academic knowledge provided support for our vision and it helped open our minds to new ideas to develop our skills. Education continues to be a very important factor in building our personalities and plays an important role in developing our mental and physical skills.

Through education, we learned how to be competitive. It armed us with the tools to continue to enrich our minds with knowledge. Education gave us opportunities to open many closed doors that prevented us from thriving. We became open to acknowledge our limitations and developed well-organized, useful techniques to adapt and cope with training in our garage. We transformed our perception of the garage as our gym and into our lab, the only motivational place where we train and flourish.

Education allowed us to open many closed doors that prevented us from thriving.

We began to focus our attention on two main goals: perfecting our academic performance and overcoming our limitations. It was an arduous and painful journey, especially when we had limited opportunities—given our inability to train with others and the complete solitude we experienced in our garage. Winning competitions wasn't as important as just getting into these competitions. Our former master wanted to restrict our resources so we could not grow, but we decided to shift our focus to growing in a different arena: Education. We were determined to find the keys to those closed doors through our academic performance and excellence.

During that time, the new coach offered us private lessons on Saturdays, so we could train with him for more than just one hour with the team on Friday nights. Unfortunately, things didn't go as planned. The traveling was difficult, the training techniques he used were the same every time, we did not have the opportunity to compete with top-level athletes, and it was expensive. So, we started limiting our visits to the new coach's dojo. The coach was not very happy with this idea, but he kept us as part of the team so we could provide him with the monthly tuition. He suggested doing Zoom training with the team, which we thought was a good idea and would give us plenty of time on the weekend to rest and focus on our academic performance at school.

Unfortunately, the Zoom training increased our stress level and made training in the garage all the more isolating and painful. We were vacillating between our hopes and our disappointments. The more hopeful we were, the more likely we would constantly be betrayed and disappointed by others.

CHAPTER SEVEN
Our Story with Pain (Jonah)

Pain is a contradictory term. Pain can exacerbate grief and magnify depression. However, our story with pain was very different. Pain accompanied us for so long that it became exceptionally familiar. We saw our pain, felt our pain, and swallowed our pain. Our story of pain was one of analysis and adaptation—we came to understand our pain, examined our painful feelings, and learned how to deal with those feelings. We built a strong mindset to protect our minds and our souls from negative thoughts that may arise inside us due to our pain. We devised a plan to resist and arm ourselves with positive thoughts. We told ourselves that we needed to dig deep within to find our potential and discover the powerful world that lay within us. We needed to dig deep within ourselves to find our inner strength. We understood we must use our potential, ability, and strength to achieve our goals and overcome our obstacles. We knew we had a powerful force within us, and that we needed to empower our vibrant, fearless inner energy.

Our parents consistently taught us to be determined, fight for our beliefs, and to face our fears. Mom and dad raised us to be independent, follow what we believe is right, value to all we do, and give gratitude for all that we have. We believed in our sport and focused our attention on mastering it, despite all the obstacles we faced and the limitations we were surrounded by in our garage. In our garage training, we saw a one-time show and a once-in-a-lifetime opportunity to shape our identity and our future. We viewed striving to find our limits as an assessment of our strong mental capacity, as well as, a test of the highest level of patience we were able to reach. At that time, training in our garage was a journey we didn't choose to embark upon but one that we understood we had to accept.

We had to hold on to hope, but we couldn't stop our childhood innocence from disappearing on account of our former master and his influence on others. We felt as if our childhood souls were dying and that our youth was slipping away. Regarding our beloved sport, we were ten-year-old kids left alone in the deep, dark, unknown forest without professional guidance and without the skills to survive. We walked down that shadowy path alone, holding our brave little hearts in our chests with little hope of survival. We were forced to take responsibility over our own success at a young age.

Our encounters with pain was a story of a "frenemy." Pain took a vow to keep us company during every moment of our lives. Pain fed us daily. We breathed the pain, we cried from the pain, and we laughed with the pain. It became the new norm in our lives; a norm to which we were forced to adapt and endure.

Every time we entered our gloomy garage, we would see our pain staring at us, sitting in the corner of the garage, joyfully observing our daily struggles. Our story of pain was about hope, disappointment, hate, love, strength, weakness, illusions, truths, revenge, forgiveness, dreams, and truth. It is a story of the many contradictions that invaded our lives and shook our core. Pain drained our energy and shattered our strength. We would enter our garage daily to train, while pulling along whatever was left of our fighting spirit, as we refused to let go of the pain that continually followed behind us. We faced our pain with dignity and began our battle with honor. We were ready to fight our struggle and press our limits to defeat the enemy. We were ready to start our battle to face our weakness, break our chains, grow our wings and fly.

Into the Unknown

We all chase our dreams into the unknown, facing obstacles, challenges, and limitations along the way. But there is something inside of us that tells us not to give up, stay focused, keep trying, stay on track, and believe we have numerous shots to take if we want to grow. We have unlimited opportunities. We have profound power within ourselves, and that energy gives us the strength to overcome our obstacles. We have the power within us to heal us and make us stronger than before. This power allows us to take a leap of faith and jump into the unknown, to discover a bright, new world in which we can create with our dreams and goals. We have a power within us that allows us to dream without fear, explore without limits, and imagine without restrictions. We just need to dare to dream, dare to make those dreams happen, and dare to soar over the walls that surround us in our garage— or any other confined space.

We continued our training alone in our garage as we prepared for Canada's opening competition with a new vision and refreshed attitude. We were focused on maintaining the desired weight to fit our weight class divisions. To do so, we followed a very healthy diet. We adopted a new technique to maintain our faith—stay positive and see our obstacles as opportunities. We pushed ourselves to amplify the positivity around us and strengthen our will to succeed. We had suffered enough in the face of difficulties, obstacles, limitations, and bullying we faced. Yet without our suffering, we would not have come to this realization of our pain; we wouldn't have helped ourselves grow stronger, smarter, and healthier than before. We believed in the power of God and relied on our faith in Him.

The Canada Open was around the corner and we were ready to smash our fears and show ourselves that we could be the people we wanted to be —and that no one could use their power to get in our way. No one would limit our dreams. We would not give in to anyone who tried to fill our minds with fear and cover us with darkness. The tough challenges we experienced in the garage shaped our thoughts and behaviors. They tried to force us to give up what we had, but we chose not to give up, or give in to those concessions.

The Canadian Open was one of the most amazing competitions we had ever participated in. Our minds were clear. We didn't have any negative distractions around us. We trained hard for these matches and maintained our weight in a very healthy way. We were ready to conquer our doubts and crush our fears.

We still remember that date: September 30, 2017. We entered the holding area with passion and determination to break our chains in the ring, fight our fears, and tear down our walls. We entered the ring to win—to win our fight against the pain that was holding us back. We wanted to be victorious in our battle against our former master. We wanted to fly beyond where his power and authority had reached. In victory, we wanted to beat the fear living inside ourselves, and start a new life free from pain and fear. Our strong will to win was decisively changed our lives that day. We were driven by the desire to win and never let doubt enter our hearts or cloud our minds.

We adopted a new technique to keep us in faith—
stay positive and see our obstacles as opportunities

The Canada Open was around the corner, and we were ready to smash our fears and show ourselves that we could be the people we wanted to be and that no one could use their power to get in our way

This was the victory we dreamed of

We both came home with two shining medals
and earned back the dignity that had been stolen from us

We entered the ring to win our fight against the pain that was holding us back. We wanted to win our
battle against our former master; we wanted to fly beyond what his power and authority had reached

Canada Open, We were happy and so carried away by our victory

We both won our fights at the Canadian Open. We fought with a positive attitude and new confidence. It was the victory we dreamed of. We both came home with two shining medals and earned back the dignity that had been stolen from us.

Sitting in our hotel room the night after the competition, we looked at our medals and decided to write a letter to our pain. The words that came out, flowed smoothly from our hearts:

> "Dear Pain,
> Your shadow took over our bodies.
> We were scared to run from you.
> We were afraid to face you over and over again.
> Our voice fades away.
> Our screams filled the whole planet, but no one could hear us.
> Our hearts were bleeding quietly, and our bodies were getting weaker and weaker.
> Dear Pain,
> You took over our bodies.
> You tore us up slowly.
> You tied our legs with hopeless chains,
>   and you told us that we would always be your prisoners.
> You built dark walls around us.
> But let us tell you something…
>
> Dear Pain,
> You may have invaded our bodies, but you didn't invade our spirit.

Dear Pain,
Listen carefully to us now, as this is for you—
For teaching us the true meaning of life.
In the times of the struggle that you brought us,
    you've also given us pleasure.
In the drops of tears, you caused,
    you brought us oceans of opportunities.
With all the doors that you closed for us,
    you brought us windows that led our dreams into becoming
    a reality.
In all the darkness you covered us up with,
    you lit up our hearts with hope.
In all the doubt you gave us,
    you brought confidence and dignity.
You pushed us over the edge,
    so we could learn to fly.

**We felt our childhood souls were dying
and our youth was slipping away**

Dear Pain,
You forgot to kill the dreams and hopes streaming in our veins.
You forget to weaken our will.
You forgot to wipe out the strength from our minds.
Let us tell you something, Pain —
We fired up the last tiny flame that was inside our hearts again.
We drew a new bridge to walk across.
We forced our eyes to see the light through the darkness
    you covered us with.
We broke the heavy chains you tied around our legs.
    and we became free.

We opened our wings wide and we flew high,
    high up to the sky–
    where we see you as small and where we can touch the stars.
We released the strength inside of us and
    the willpower inside of us.
We saw you fade away because of the bright light inside our hearts.

Dear Pain,
Look at us now dancing with the stars,
    hearing our voices getting louder and louder, telling you,
At times, we thought you won. But it turned out that the battle
    hadn't even started.
You've brought us many obstacles, but we learned how to
    overcome them.

Dear Pain,
You made a mistake by choosing us.
You made a mistake by invading us.
Because through our struggles, we learned how to be strong.
We learned how to stand up for ourselves, how to defend ourselves.
Because we are unbreakable,
    because we are eagles,
    and the eagles have soared.

During our daily training in the garage—
We try to overcome feelings of rejection and isolation to focus on our goal

Dear Pain, you took over our bodies. First, you tore us up slowly—
Then, you tied our legs with hopeless chains and told us that we would always be your prisoners

Our screams filled the whole planet, but no one could hear us

Pain invaded our hearts and chained our souls with heavy chains

The pain slowly tore us apart

We pledged to keep our promise and work hard, overcome our obstacles
and reach the world championship; no matter what we face, we will keep moving forward

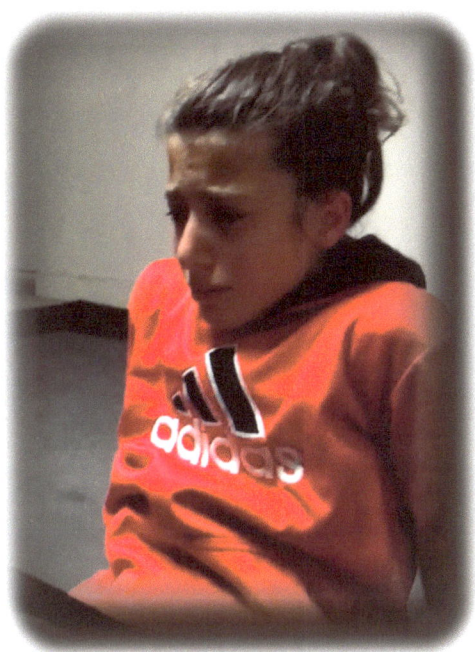

Our hearts were bleeding quietly,
and our bodies were getting weaker and weaker

Our story of pain was about hope, disappointment, hate, love, strength, weakness, illusions, truths, revenge, forgiveness, and dreams. A tale of many contradictions invaded our lives and shook our cores.

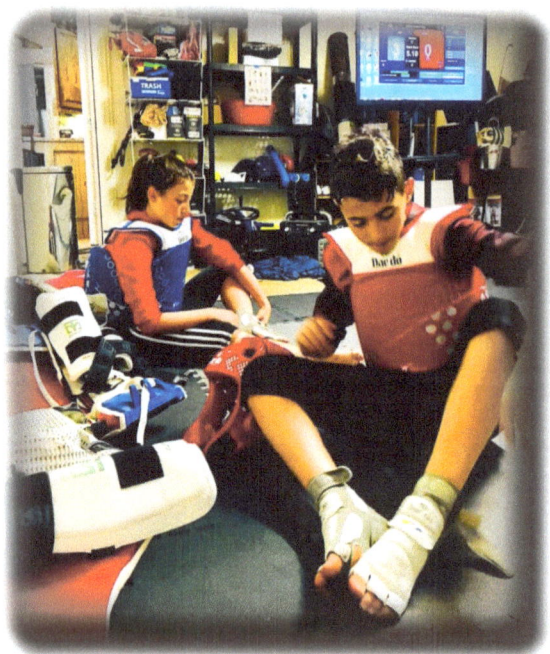

Garage training, preparing for competition, trying to beat our pain

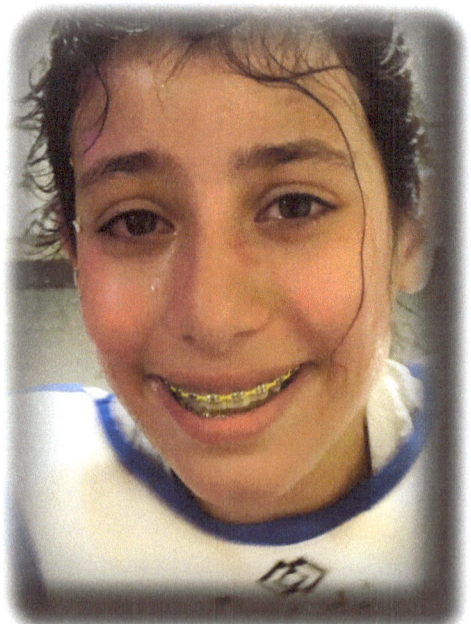

Pain brought us many obstacles, But we have learned how to overcome them

Shadows of pain covered our souls with despair

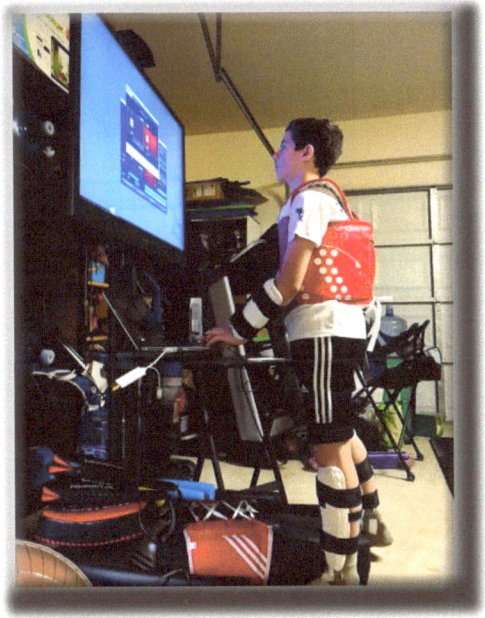

We have taken control of our garage training
by taking full responsibility for achieving our goal

Garage training was painful to experience; pain built dark walls around us. We felt despair, devastated, and covered in pain

We had to hold on to hope but couldn't stop our childhood innocence from disappearing because of our former master and his influence on others. We felt our childhood souls were withering and our youth was slipping away

Rejection is Harsh (Sally)

We were excited to train right after the Canadian Open and the great success we had. We continued our training alone in our garage and were full of positivity. Our next competition was the President's Cup at the Taekwondo Federation President's Championship. We had less than a month to prepare for this competition, which is one of the most prestigious tournaments in the world. We knew we needed to perform at our best in these matches, especially since the World Taekwondo President would be there. We will never forget how kind and supportive he was when he wrote about our story in the World Taekwondo Federation webpage and magazine, followed by a gift the federation sent us, after he saw the interview we had at the State Championship.

The tournament was held in Las Vegas. We got there early so we could adjust the cutting of our weight at the last minute. Conditions at the arena seemed strange at the time. We felt uncomfortable seeing our old team members, our former master, and several coaches who were among those that turned us away. Many questioning, cold eyes followed us wherever we went. We were still so young, but this time, the feeling of rejection that had hurt us before was not able to spoil our mood, or mess with our minds. We accepted the rejection and focused on achieving our goal. We knew we had to win to eliminate any chances of them criticizing or insulting us. We needed this victory to formally announce our identities. The President's Cup wasn't just another tournament for us. It was our ticket to freedom.

Our new coach arrived with his team and business partner. It was their chance to show that their team and dojo were strong, and they needed to build a name among the many good dojos across the country. Although the coach was an Olympic coach, this situation was different, as he had built up his new team as a business, after leaving his job as a national team coach for one of the foreign national teams. The dojo was his retirement project.

At this competition, Jonah emerged as a new version of himself; he was full of emotion and brimming with positivity. He won his five fights and was in complete control of his mind. We both won our battles and earned our medals through our hard work. We were so excited about our victories and the opportunity to stand triumphant in front of all of those who had rejected us. We ran toward the main podium where the World Taekwondo President was sitting and showed him our medals. He was very kind and nice to us. After congratulating us, he told us that he had a strong feeling he would be seeing us again—but this time at the World Cadet Championships. We took his words very seriously and set another goal for ourselves: to get accepted to the World Cadet Championships.

We needed this win to announce our identities formally

Jonah emerged as a new version of himself; he was full of emotion and brimming with positivity — He won his five fights and was in control of his mind

After congratulating us, the president of the World Taekwondo Federation told us that he had a strong feeling that he would be seeing us again, but this time at the World Cadet Championships.

We were excited about our victories and the opportunity to stand triumphant in front of all who rejected us. We ran toward the main podium, where the World Taekwondo President sat, and showed him our medals.

We both won our battles and earned our medals through our hard work

We were so excited about our victories and the opportunity to stand triumphant in front of those who rejected us

Zoom training with the new Olympic coach had become a huge headache. We were not able to communicate well with the coach via Zoom. His explanations of the exercises were not clear to us, and his instructions were directed to the team in the room with him, without consideration for us—as the kind of workouts they were doing needed more space and more partners than we had in our garage. We felt neglected, as if no one had taken into account our situation. We began getting frustrated, especially when the coach kept forgetting to log onto Zoom, requiring us to keep calling him to switch on the camera, so we could join the training. There were times that no one would even answer our calls and we would have to continue the training session alone!

Furthermore, this training time was taking time away from our schoolwork. We valued our time and needed to ensure we were learning. Unfortunately, these problematic Zoom classes began to negatively affect our passion for training. It took us less than two months to recognize the negative impact these online sessions were having on our hearts and minds. We asked our parents to cancel the training membership via Zoom. Although they didn't want us to be alone, and had hoped that this form of training would at least provide emotional support, they agreed to discontinue the training over Zoom. The new coach seemed OK with stopping the Zoom training, as we were the only athletes that hadn't quit the online learning. Our parents kept paying the monthly membership fee, nevertheless, in exchange for Jonah and me remaining part of the team.

We continued to train by ourselves in our garage, but we returned to the new coach's dojo every weekend, because he had asked if we would participate in some Friday night sparring sessions with his team to help them out. It was hard for us to travel after a long day at school. We'd arrive at the dojo in the late afternoon, quickly change into our training clothes, and immediately jump into his team's practice session. Jonah and I partnered with each other for warm-up training, because everyone already had a partner. None of the team players spoke to us, just the adults did. We didn't feel like we belonged. Nevertheless, we still felt compelled to travel all the way there each week to train with the coach for less than an hour and come home early in the morning the next day. It was not only about the expense our parents incurred, but also the time we invested and hours we wasted those many weekends on the road.

Our parents came from a culture built on respect and values; essential principles of character which they conveyed to us. Therefore, we all felt an imperative to stand by the new coach. We accepted being on his team, even though we knew he only wanted money, because we respected that he allowed us to be listed under his team's name. We appreciated the opportunity he afforded us and were ready to help the rest of his team grow.

Traveling to join the new Olympic coach and his team for Friday sparring sessions was toughest for our mom, since our dad was busy with work and traveled a lot. But, we continued going every weekend until we had a terrible car accident on our way one Friday. My mom lost control of the car after the front tire exploded. Our car flipped up and down four times until it got stuck in a stream off the side of the road. Several cars stopped and tried to help us get out of the car as glass had shattered all over us. The ambulance took us to the hospital and did several x-rays to see if we had any broken bones. Fortunately none of us were physically injured. However, it took us a while to get over this traumatic experience. In fact, since that day our mother still cannot drive to go to that dojo. She developed a phobia of driving, and it took a while for her to recover.

After the accident, we continued our training in our garage and stopped going to the dojo, but we continued to pay monthly tuition. Our parents didn't want to open another door to conflict, because they knew that the moment we stopped paying tuition, the Olympic coach would turn his back on us, and we would add more enemies to the list. Our family placed a larger value on our collective peace of mind, over the wasted tuition fees, as we could not bear to endure any more pain.

Traveling to join the new Olympic coach and his team for Friday sparring sessions was challenging for our mom since our dad was busy with work and traveled a lot. But, we continued going every weekend until we had a terrible car accident on our way on Friday

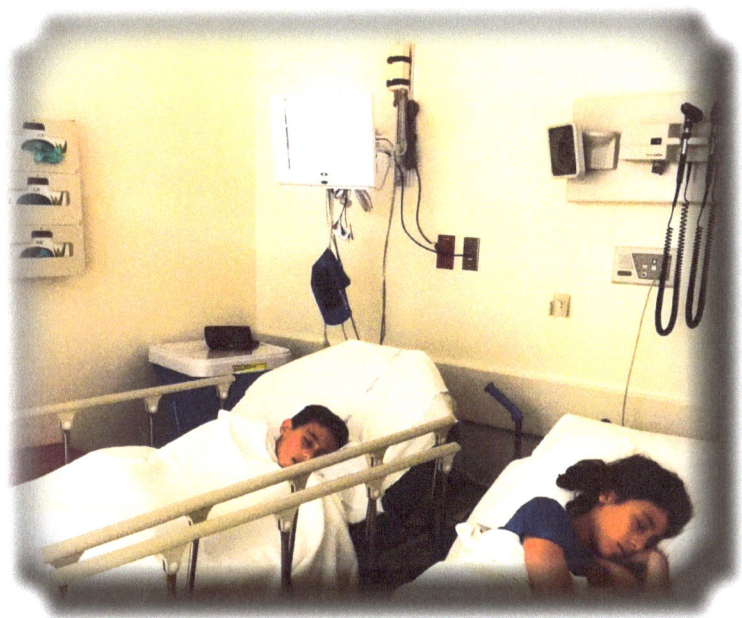

Jonah and I were in the hospital after the car accident; another traumatic experience added fear and pain to our hearts and minds

During this time, the State Taekwondo Federation organized a very rigorous training camp led by a well-known Olympic champion from a European country. Working alongside the Olympic champion were two national team coaches. This was a great opening for us to expand our training and gain some new skills. We saw this as a tremendous opportunity—a one-time showcase of very challenging training techniques, as well as the chance to train with a diverse group of athletes for three full days. Although we were nervous about going to camp because all the athletes and coaches across the country would be there (including the ones that turned us away), we were no longer afraid. We thought that surely no one will dare harass us in front of top-level coaches and Olympic athletes. Sadly, we were wrong. We had once again underestimated our former master's influence. What should have been a day of learning and skill training overseen by the state administration became yet another day of painful humiliation that left us with a profound sadness that we carried in our hearts for so long.

Will the Negativity Ever Stop?

In the early morning of October 28, 2017, we left our house and headed to the neighboring city where the training camp was being held. The Vice President of the Taekwondo Federation and one of our former master's best friends were hosting the training camp in the Grand Dojo.

We arrived early enough to pay the camp entrance fee and start the stretching routine. As we sat inside the Grand Dojo, our parents sat on little benches by the large glass windows just outside. The athletes and coaches began to arrive, and the dojo started to crowd with cold, familiar faces. At the time, we were just 11 years old, though we were treated like adults—not based on nods of respect, but with the decisive intent to ignore and humiliate. Nevertheless, we gathered our strength and whispered in each other's ears to keep moving forward, focus on the task at hand, and erase all those negative voices from our heads. We knew we must remain positive and be who we are despite the antagonistic forces that threatened our calm and our confidence. We needed to take a deep breath and trust ourselves.

Mastering our attention required substantial willpower. Strong willpower allowed us to intentionally ignore distractions while staying focused on the task at hand. Finally, we needed to bolster our trust in each other, our mission, together with our trust in the process. Trust breeds unity, and unity leads to prosperity.

The boot camp started with the coaches and the Olympic champion. We were so excited to be a part of this training and felt like we were living the normal life, just like the rest of the athletes. What an awesome opportunity! But, as we looked around at the many familiar faces of the athletes, we recognized they did not seem to understand how lucky they were to be there. They were unable to appreciate the little things in life, even something as small as the privilege of participating in a boot camp—as they all had regular dojos and coaches to work with, as well as friends with whom to train. We had hoped to get a chance to partner with new athletes and practice with a variety of kids. Unfortunately, we ended up training only with each other. It was a quiet disappointment for us, but was to be expected. Our former master had defamed our reputation and made us look like we had a contagious disease. Once again, we were faced with stereotypes based on biases and lies. The integrity, discipline, and respect our sport was supposed to radiate were absent in our former master and his allies.

Disappointment was our close friend; we had become accustomed to it and it had become a part of our journey. We knew we couldn't change people's behaviors or negative forces if they didn't want to change. We could only control our reaction and attitude toward these behaviors and forces. So, we decided we should follow our plan: we would ignore any distractions around us, block our ears from hearing negative voices, and get the most we could out of this camp.

Our motto at that moment became to see every obstacle as an opportunity to grow. We hardly ever went to camps or trained with others, so we would have to do our best to direct our focus toward achieving our goal, and eliminate any unnecessary emotional outbursts that may arise from various unprofessional behaviors of any of the many coaches. These coaches targeted us. They targeted our confidence, our self-esteem, and our inner peace. They tried to make us lose our temper as a result of how much humiliation we encountered there—but we wouldn't give them what they wanted. Training in solitude for so many years in our garage had enabled our minds and hearts to work together in harmony. We had learned how to hide our pain and calm our anger. Our journey in the garage wasn't just a physical exercise for our bodies. In that garage, we had learned how to train our souls, spirits, and minds. We had learned how to turn negative emotions into positive ones. Training in the garage was the main reason we became mentally and emotionally more mature than our peers. Living in solitude sent us on a unique journey that exposed us to difficult challenges that taught us how to develop techniques, skills, and methods to overcome obstacles. We insisted on continuing to train in our garage—not to win medals or go to competitions, but to face our fears and weaknesses and cultivate the mental strength that would help us focus on what matters most to us: our education and future careers.

There was a plan by these coaches to push us to our limits and make us collapse. We were alone in the middle of the crowd. We were sad and disappointed, but remained unafraid to face them. There is a big difference between feeling disappointed or sad, and being afraid. We were not afraid, however, we were disappointed and saddened by what these coaches did to us.

Our last day of the training camp was a turning point in our perception of our sport. It began as any normal morning. We headed to training camp ready to conquer the day. We were full of positivity and hope, but things began to take another direction the moment our eyes fell on our former master. He was wearing the same shirt worn by both coaches and State officials. He was part of the training camp squad. Our parents held our hands tightly and looked at us warmly as they confidently told us to be strong and not to be afraid. "We're here for you. Don't worry about him. He's weaker than he looks," were our father's words to us.

We began to feel the pressure our former master had on the other coaches the moment we entered the dojo. We felt as if a tornado had come and destroyed everything. We walked through the dojo pretending to be strong and avoiding looking at him, but the moment we passed him we heard a scary sound whispering to us, and I (Sally) immediately lost control over my feelings. I began to shiver. I tried to gather what was left of my strength. Taking lopsided steps, I rushed all the way out of the dojo. Jonah followed me, with a heavy heart and a hopeless face, looking as if he had lost something precious. I can still remember my mom's face when we got close to her. Mom's face displayed such despair; her strong, confident personality weakened when she saw our pain. She tried to gather her strength and immediately took us to the restroom to freshen up. I felt dizzy and nauseous and couldn't stand by myself. I wasn't scared, but I felt depressed, overwhelmed, and speechless. We told our parents what our former master had said to us as we passed by him. They were very hurtful and insulting words, the same ones he always used in his dojo, but this time he followed them up by calling us "losers."

We sat with our parents outside the dojo and looked at our former master and a group of coaches who were laughing and enjoying their time together. It's like nothing happened; not a single coach approached us and asked us what happened, why we were sitting outside and not training, or even if we were feeling well.

We felt like strangers; we didn't belong in this boot camp. We no longer felt that our sport emphasized discipline, principle, and integrity. How were these coaches masters of this sport? We were disappointed by our sports role models and were also sad to be in that environment. The conflict within us increased. We struggled between gathering our training gear and leaving the training camp or gathering our strength and continuing our training. If we left, we would be giving our former master what he wanted. We would be allowing him to destroy our confidence, block our path, and limit the way forward. In contrast, if we entered the dojo and continued our training with strength and power, we would conquer him and repair our dignity. Our struggle was between negative and positive forces, but which one would triumph? The choice was ours, and we had to decide wisely.

Over the course of our three-year struggle training alone in our garage, we learned that through action and reaction we can grasp how to develop our skills. The beauty of struggling to defeat the obstacles we encounter is that doing so reactivates the power within us. How we act and react to the hurdles in our path determines how we conquer them. We must be quick, but we must control our attitude toward the hardships we face. We are always mindful that we can't control the behaviors of others, and that how others decide to behave does not determine how we react. It is our choice to follow the esteemed principles of our sport, demonstrate our discipline, and take the high road when others decide to lose sight of their self-respect.

Insults were the weapon our former master used to target our confidence and destroy our reputation. But, we had finally developed our own weapon to resist our former master; a weapon that would help us win the fight, maintain our respect for the sport, as well as the principles and discipline our sport had taught us. We would not give our former master what he wants. Instead, we had to clear our minds. We always believed that repetition bolsters determination. Through repetition, we become stronger and smarter so that every time our former master targets our confidence we become even more determined to continue our journey and reach our goal. Success is our identity.

Thoughts are Power

Our thoughts are very powerful, and we must control what happens inside our minds. Through balance we can focus, but we must choose what we focus on. Therefore, we need to continually enable the positivity within us, continue to develop, growing smarter, stronger, and more powerful than before, as we face our former master.

We hugged our parents, wiped away our tears, and told them not to worry about us, because we felt so much better than we had before. Our parents are the most phenomenal support system any child could want or need. They have always believed in us and supported our decisions. They taught us to take full responsibility for our lives—because if we succeed, the success is ours; and if we fail, the failure is also ours. Most importantly, they taught us to never give up.

We entered the dojo. As we passed our former master we looked confidently and directly into his eyes and smiled softly. It was our smiles that killed the negativity and allowed positivity to blossom. This was the beginning of a new chapter; a chapter in which *we* would write the story—our story, our journey. Our lives would be lives of victory, hope, and triumph.

That same day, we explained to the Vice President of the State Taekwondo Organization everything that had happened. As we expected, the Vice President dismissed our story and sided with our former master— which was the reaction we expected from someone who had agreed to be part of an unprovoked war against two children, from the start. However, what was unexpected was the reaction of one of the coaches who was a partner of the Olympic coach whose dojo we were still associated with at the time. This coach refused to stand by us and told our parents, "Yes, they are our students, but we cannot support them in public, because our business is new and we need to avoid any issues that may arise from going against their former master. Our dojo's name could be hurt due to this conflict."

The remarks made to us that day by our former master were profoundly painful. But hearing that self-absorbed, heartless statement from someone who knows we are part of his team was heart-wrenching. That coach knew the agony we had gone through. He had offered us a place on his team, and a chance to be his students. Furthermore, even if we didn't train with the rest of his students, we still paid the same tuition! We were young children, we were athletes participating in a sport that espouses the imperative to stand up against bullying and abuse. Coaches demand that their students respect each other and act with discipline— so how dare he speak of respect and discipline if he has no sense of respect for us as athletes? How dare he demand respect from any of his students? At that moment, we realized the principles of our sport were an illusion living in our minds and hearts. That was when all the masks fell off and what remained were the true faces of these coaches. That day we realized that people wear as many masks as they can or need to hide their true identities.

CHAPTER EIGHT
The Process: Finding our Rhythm (Jonah)

Encountering obstacles is essential to mental development. It is through overcoming these obstacles that we learn to push ourselves beyond our comfort zone. More importantly, confronting obstacles teaches us skills that we cannot learn from other experiences in our lives, like: how to develop our faith; how to stay positive; how we see everything around us reflecting bright light even if it is dark; and how to be happy on the inside.

During our daily practices in our garage, we came to a point at which we couldn't keep avoiding our obstacles. We needed to respond to our bullies, but on our terms and not theirs. What happened to us in the previous year—and especially at the statewide Taekwondo camp—taught us that we had to find another path that would lead us to achieve our goals and overcome our limitations. Our sport is riddled with corruption, discrimination, and racism. Many coaches use their platforms to ruin the lives of athletes just because they don't follow their policies. Masters manipulate other athletes and coaches by using the power given to them based on their position. They were using a sport built on integrity, respect, and discipline in a very disappointing way.

We needed to stop focusing on the negativity we encountered, which was bigger than us and could lead us to many disappointments. Surrendering to negativity could kill every beautiful vision we had. We needed to look inward toward ourselves and our sport. We had to think intelligently and triumph over the negativity with our abilities and knowledge. We needed to think outside the box, even though we were prisoners inside an actual box—our garage. We had to use our education, our knowledge, and our intellect to create peaceful weapons that could be used to end negativity. Passion is the master of all success. While in the garage, we reminded ourselves daily to never stop dreaming, for the moment we stop, we will die as human beings, students, children, and athletes.

Our motivation was no longer about medals, podiums, achievements, sports, or rewards—it was about our identity, existence, free will, human rights, freedom, and the strength of our minds. The most important battle we needed to win was the one within our heads; the struggle that had conquered our hearts and the stumbling blocks our former master placed in our path. We must trust the process and believe in ourselves. We must strengthen our belief in God, His greatness, His justice, and His plan for us. We knew that we have a powerful force within us that can help us overcome our difficulties, achieve our goals, and conquer our fears. We just needed to strengthen our belief in our abilities, even if everyone else doubted us. We had only ourselves to count on. If we believed in the power within us, we would have the courage to live our dreams despite the darkness that surrounded us.

Music Is Power

Garage training helped us shatter our limitations and defeat our obstacles. Simplicity was a concept that we adapted to pave our path and relieve our pain. Simplicity emphasizes focus. It grants us full command over our journey, clearing our minds and giving us full control to lead ourselves on the desired path. The more we simplified our obstacles, troubles, and challenges, the more we would have an easy journey. Through simplicity, we were able to listen to our hearts and speak to our minds. It felt like a bridge was built between our rational and emotional judgment, and a beautiful and smooth harmony flowed between the two. Our seamless communication sounded like a beautiful song; we listened to it passionately and danced with joy.

We finally realized that we had found our rhythm in life. Dancing is the art of movement; it came to us in different ways and added meaning to our moves. Dancing allowed us to reflect on our inner emotions and open the path to expanding our power to create. We chose to dance as it is meaningful, full of power, and reflected our inner strength. We had to learn how to move our feet smoothly to avoid the negativity and obstacles in front of us. We needed to dance to our rhythm to grow faster, stronger, healthier, and smarter.

Music was our magic wand. We used music to open mysterious pathways within us that were not known to us before. We listened to music that spoke to our minds and motivated our hearts to beat with an extraordinary passion that ignited our determination to keep going and move forward. We found the magic within the music and used it to strike our obstacles and shatter the ghost of darkness living in the depths of our hearts. Music brought life to the garage and changed our mood. We listened daily to music. We sang and danced while practicing alone in our home garage. Music transformed our perception of our garage: through music, we saw a bright window to our freedom among the dark walls, and we smiled through the dusty air. Music showed us the purity and fertility of our talents and a new life for the rebirth of our identities.

Action and Reaction

Through action and reaction, we learn how to develop our skills. The beauty of overcoming our struggles lies in reactivating the power within us. The way we act and deal with our obstacles determines how we conquer them; we must be quick and in control of our mood. We have the inner strength to have complete control over our attitude toward the barriers we encounter.

Our awareness of the usual, strange atmosphere in our garage collided with a new, different look and feel during the long time we spent there, over the course of the many hours we had been training our minds to learn how to dance. Working hard on studying our mental and physical proficiency gave us the essential qualities to train ourselves to think more rationally about our setbacks. We found ways to turn our garage training into a laboratory in which we could examine, and study in-depth, how far our minds could go; how far we could reach and evolve. Our vision and way of thinking were taken to a higher level, redirecting our minds to explore our inner strength and examine the growth of our mindset. We focused on raising our physical abilities by elevating our mental capabilities.

Our examination of our situation was based on our full understanding of our limitations. We realized that the moment we reached the edge of our comfort zone, we would be able to raise our sense of being to a higher level. We would be able to face our fears, face the truth, and clearly see that we have no way of going back. We must push more and keep moving forward, kicking our obstacles and breaking all the barriers in our path to get to the next level, where the real journey can begin and new opportunities could open up. We needed to run fast to continually keep moving forward. We must open our eyes wide, dare to see the darkness, and dare to touch the pain. We had to stop running back to where we started and charge ahead, running independently.

We realized that the moment we reached the edge of our comfort zone, we could raise our sense of being to a higher level

We found ways to turn our garage training into a laboratory in which we could examine and study in-depth how far our minds could go, and how far we could reach and evolve

We focused on raising our physical abilities by elevating our mental capabilities

We expanded our capabilities through resistance

We've leveled up our fighting techniques by challenging each other's abilities and studying how our brains can operate in highly stressful scenarios

When we witness the birth of our inner strength through struggle, we encounter powerful forces stronger than ourselves, and our failure to overcome our obstacles gives us a purpose to continue.

The Rise of Inner Strength

The beauty of our contest lies in the process we go through. When we witness the birth of our inner strength, through struggle; we encounter powerful forces stronger than ourselves. Our failure to overcome our obstacles gives us purpose to continue. Through this process, we can reach the ultimate realization of our strength. Our obstacles serve as our motivation to overcome our limitations.

We all go through ups and downs, feeling intense emotions that make us angry, sad, and frustrated, though in the end, we feel proud. We take pride in discovering a world within us, a world of possibility and growth. We fight hard to open doors that were closed before. We will see how the power of positivity can conquer fears, remove doubts, defeat obstacles, and allow us to reach our goals. Our ultimate goal is being able to solve the mystery sources of our inner strength.

Living in the garage for the first three years of our journey was a story of struggle and defeat; entering the garage for training after a long day at school was our daily challenge. We trained for more than two hours a day in both the bitter cold of the winter and the extreme heat of the summer. We hated every minute in the garage, but loved the opportunity God gave us to build mutual trust between our minds, and our hearts. There was no doubt in our hearts that our suffering was the result of a Divine, unrevealed cause. We believed in our destiny and came to a certain level of realization that there was a purpose behind our struggle. We sought answers to the many questions that went through our heads. Why were we so stubborn, insisting to live through this pain? Why didn't we just give up? Why didn't we switch to another sport, or stop participating in any sport and just live the rest of our lives in joy and peace?

Stubbornness is a Power!

Our stubbornness confirmed our desire to continue the journey despite all the hardships we encountered. It was a positive trait we possess and played a critical role in strengthening our mental defense mechanisms. Stubborn determination was a powerful motivator that keep us thriving.

We appreciated the reward we got every time we beat our challenges. As kids, it wasn't easy for us to understand why we had to train in the garage. We had no clue what crime we had been suspected of committing to deserve such punishment. We were forced into our garage as if we were prisoners under the authority of a corrupt and abusive warden. During the first three years of our training, we were plagued by unexplained disappointments and afflicted by unexplained anger, hatred, low expectations, and humiliation. Yet, every experience we went through shaped our character and cleared our vision. We forced ourselves to expand our abilities, pressured our minds to grow; choosing confrontation over running and hiding.

Without proper control over our motor skills, we would be unable to apply our strength and flexibility in desired ways. We developed our motor skills, increased our sense of self-movement, and learned more about body position. Although we had given our minds complete control over our body's capacities and capabilities, we needed maturity to overcome the obstacles and limitations we faced; so we could set higher prospects for ourselves, and work persistently to meet those unrealistic expectations.

The Spread

Through the obstacles we faced, we have learned to take ourselves out of our comfort zone and discover new abilities. Perhaps most importantly, our obstacles taught us how to dig deep within ourselves and reveal our greatest power: our inner strength. Conquering obstacles taught us who we really are. We were able to see ourselves as undefeated and unbreakable. We'd been through three years of pain, humiliation, and mental abuse—and now, for the first time, were finally beginning to see how strong we were and how secure we were in our abilities.

We changed our perception of ourselves the moment we changed our thinking; empowering the power of the "I" within us and charging our minds with positive energy. We began repeating empowering words to ourselves to strengthen our belief in one another. How powerful we felt when we heard ourselves repeating these potent phrases over and over again inside our minds! "I am God's masterpiece." "I am His creation." "I am unbreakable, undefeated, and strong."

There is always a new beginning at every opportunity. We have seen the unlimited possibilities that we can create with new beginnings. Hope always lives in unbreakable hearts, and hope had been our only friend during the difficult times we faced during our garage isolation. Through hope, we saw new opportunities within our obstacles. There are always obstacles, challenges, limitations, and setbacks along the way, but there was also always a light of hope—a bright, positive star that could light the darkness we felt in the garage. Using our limitations as fuel to increase our speed toward our growth potential was one useful technique that we employed to survive training in our garage.

We saw our strength in our obstacles. We empowered the strength within us to conquer our limitations by overcoming our obstacles. We have been able to take the initiative and control the barriers that were supposed to compel us to quit. We believed we had the power within us to explore our capabilities, expand our journey, strengthen our mentality, and overcome the limitations pushing to force us to give up. We traveled thousands of miles, deep in our minds, searching for mysterious power, hoping for a chance to survive. We withstood our bullies and obstacles, and we didn't stop exploring until we found a treasure within us. We possessed the strength to open new doors to new opportunities to achieve our goals and dreams. We refused to underestimate our strength, and we unlocked the door and opened it wide to free our souls from the prison in which we were dying. Our wings widened, and we flew high, up to the sky where we could see our pain, and where we could catch the stars.

CHAPTER NINE
Positivity is a Choice (Sally)

Positivity is the quality of having an optimistic attitude while living through an endless series of battles with darkness. Positivity was a behavior that we forced ourselves to adapt to survive our pain and overcome our obstacles. It was not an easy path to take or an easy decision to make— especially after the bad experiences we had with our former master, along with the multiple and repeated rejection we endured at the hands of many coaches and dojos in our sport.

    We felt desperate, as we started to notice the rise of negative feelings inside us. Injustice had overshadowed our dreams, and hatred began to find its way into our hearts. We couldn't continue carrying the animosity that lived within us toward everyone who had caused us pain. We could not remain stuck in a stage that would not allow us to grow. We knew that our previous master's obsession with shattering our dream continued getting stronger. Moreover, we were aware that our negative feelings about the relentless injustice we encountered were getting stronger, as well. Accordingly, we both felt the hatred burning; the one feeling we were trying to avoid. Attempting to avoid offending our former master, despite his persistent bullying and the pain he caused us daily, was not healthy for us. Our former master was everywhere and had abundant ways of manipulating others to hurt us. He erroneously thought we were too weak to defend ourselves. We were constantly trying to evade him, move on, focus on our training and invest in our future plans—but, unfortunately, he refused to leave us alone. His obsession with destroying us had become a disease that threatened us. We looked for ways to sever the roots of hatred from our hearts and in its place instill forgiveness and love. We needed to look at our former master with sympathy. He needed immediate help, because there is no reason for a healthy and normal human being, especially an adult, to be obsessed with inflicting pain and suffering on two children unless he was struggling with an internal, unstable emotional conflict.

    Once we began to adapt to the idea of looking at him with sympathy, and feeling sorry for him, it transformed our mental state from weak to strong. We felt emboldened and finally recognized our worth. His obsession with our destruction opened our eyes and minds to logic. Our former master was afraid, yet certain, that we would succeed without him—for that reason he was obsessed with trying to destroy us, obstructing our way, and repeatedly spreading rumors about us. If we succeeded and went far, it would showcase our talent and ability and leave him far behind. We understood his intentions and goals. He needed us to suffer and live in pain to win the battle. We had to overturn his plans.

Our former master's ego was his enemy; an ego that prevented him from seeing his faults. We felt he wanted to see us suffer and feel worthless without him. So to win our battle against him we had to reverse these plans. It was time to gather our strength; take command over our mindset and reclaim our dream. Even in the darkest of times, we must hold on to optimism, which will add light to the darkness. We must forgive to live.

The year 2018 was one of significant growth for us. It was the year that we decided to let our pain go and focus on our growth. Attempting to avoid the forces of negativity didn't work; they just followed us everywhere we went. We decided that the only way out of our unbearable situation was a confrontation; we needed to face our obstacles, our limitations, and the forces of negativity that were trying to push us over the edge.

After a year full of suffering, we had to change our plan and our techniques. Whatever battle we were going to have this year had to be on our terms. We had suffered enough during the past three years through rejection, bullying, as well as mental and emotional abuse. We had faced evil through many defeated battles, and understood we needed to change our fight strategy to succeed.

Forgiveness is a Power

Over the course of the past three years we had lived through many ups and downs. Although we had overcome numerous battles against fear and doubt, we also lost many battles to keep our childhood safe. We had fortified our mental strength, conquered abundant obstacles, and broken our chains, but our childhood was battling alongside us on the frontline, struggling to defeat monsters and ruthless forces. As a result, we lost our childhood and were left with a multitude of unhealed scars; wounds that shaped the new path we take today.

We continued training alone in our garage. We were preparing for our next tournament, the U.S. Open Taekwondo Championship, one of the biggest world tournaments. Although we were training hard, we needed to hone our abilities.

The Olympic coach offered for us to join sparring sessions with his team at his dojo. Driving more than four hours on the weekend to benefit from less than an hour of training time before heading home again, was very painful for all of us. Our dad worked so hard during the week that he needed a break on the weekend to recharge; the same was true for us with our schoolwork. Traveling was stressful, with little advantage to us—especially since those Friday-night sparring sessions did not include professional athletes. However, Friday-night sessions worked well for the other team members whose parents wanted us to spare with them to sharpen their skills. Sadly, these same sessions were not challenging for us, and did not aid in improving our techniques. Furthermore, the environment at the Friday-night sparring sessions wasn't a positive experience, as some seniors were coaching other athletes from their team against us; telling them which moves to use while sparring in order to win. We felt like we were in competition with them, rather than on the same team. Even though we were officially part of the team, they never treated us that way. The team was formal in its relationship with us, and the team members were careful in their communication with our parents as well, especially with our mother as our former master had spread so many rumors about her. He made other dojos keep their distance from us and even hesitate to communicate with us.

It got to the point that we had to talk to the Olympic coach about the fact that there was no sense in us coming to the dojo, as it only helped his athletes improve, not us. We couldn't learn any new techniques or exercises and the negative environment his team created for us was too much. Finally, the Olympic coach admitted he knew what was going on, so he suggested we stay for Saturdays to take a private class with him.

We thought it would be a good idea to have a private class with the Olympic coach, but we couldn't see what lay ahead. So, we kept coming on Friday nights to have sparring sessions with the team, and stayed through Saturday for private training with the coach. Our hopes for these new training sessions were great as we thought we would learn a lot, especially with the money we were paying him. However, training with the Olympic coach turned out to be very basic, repeating the same exercises every time that we were able to do ourselves in our garage. Patience was our guide at the time. We knew we had to be patient while climbing the ladder. We were trying to give our best and follow the guidance of the Olympic coach, even though the coach's direction did not add any new benefit to our training techniques, and our we saw no progress in our skill performance.

As a result of our training situation with the Olympic coach, our dad discerned that we needed to work on developing our fighting abilities, so he bought us an electronic system that calculates points when kicked. It was the same scoring system used in high-level competitions, such as the U.S. Open. We were doing a sparring session in our garage and rehearsals to develop our kicking techniques; weight loss was going well for us, thanks to our mom, who provided us with healthy meals and snacks, while monitoring our fitness and well-being. In addition, we put extra focus on school. We had to excel academically, too as education is very important to us. Both of our parents agreed that we could continue training in our sport— if we could balance it with maintaining our academic studies.

We remember how our mother used to tell us that education is our ticket to success in life; without education, we would not know, and without knowledge, we could not create opportunities and open closed doors. We needed diverse, broad knowledge to succeed in our sport. Our daily training and sparring sessions were not accomplishing everything we needed to help us reach the level of mental and physical readiness we required for our sport. We needed a high level of education to challenge our minds, and apply that knowledge to developing techniques, along with methods of thinking that could advance our skills in our sport. So, we both participated in a daily reading that enriched us with a lot of knowledge about our bodies, muscles, and the relationship between mind and body. We began to do scientific research and gather information about our brains, body, nutrition, and physical training that aligned with our goals. We wanted to learn more about our bodies, how our minds work, and how we can embrace our mental and physical fighting abilities.

The drive to succeed in our sport was in harmony with our drive to succeed in school, and they both had a common goal: to succeed and excel. As a result, we maintained a positive attitude throughout, and our nightly training in the garage became a daily routine.

After our normal school day was over, we would stay after hours, volunteering to help teachers organize their work, arriving back home in the late afternoon. Our mom was always waiting for us in our school parking lot. She came early every day and was always there for us in her heart and mind, ready to do her part and beyond. Then, we would go home after a long, stressful day at school, eat an early dinner, study, and head to the garage for our training session. We were exhausted. Cutting weight was a very difficult experience, but we needed to be in the right weight division to match our body size.

We had just turned 11 years old, and we were small in size compared to our peers. The athletes we were supposed to fight in our 12–14-year-old division had already reached puberty. They were taller and more physically mature than us. We needed to be in the lowest weight category to make reasonable and fair matches with kids in our body size range.

Our mother would sit in the garage every night, cheering and motivating us while we trained. We needed that support and her feedback on our performance. Our mother was always charging our minds with positivity. She was our spiritual teacher, but due to her lack of knowledge of our sport, she couldn't help us with our Taekwondo practice. She had no martial arts background and always refused to give us professional advice. Therefore, she suggested that we record our training so that we could replay what we recorded to see how we did, or if there was something we needed to work on. Her advice was a turning point in our performance development. We would take breaks to sit together and work on fixing our mistakes. This opportunity would never happen if we were training with a team, and there was no coach in any dojo, of those in which we trained, who had given us the time to fix a movement or work independently on honing our individual athletic skills.

Repeating the same exercises and working hard to reach perfection made our kick movements more professional than any other athlete in any dojo around us. We would repeat the same exercises multiple times, over and over again, until we mastered them. We perfected the drills and kicks. We became experts in our sport. What a genius idea suggested by our mother! She single-handedly transformed our perception of our skill abilities and our level of technique performance. Nevertheless, we felt guilty having her sit with us in the garage during each of our training sessions, holding her camera for hours recording our workouts. Still, she never gave up on us. Her motivational spirit gave us a different outlook on our struggles; it reinforced our desire to work hard and challenge our minds to be the best version of ourselves.

The Conflict (Sally)

The U.S. Open in Las Vegas, Nevada, was around the corner. This is one of the biggest international tournaments in the World Taekwondo Federation. Many Olympic athletes come to Las Vegas from all over the world hoping to win and earn some Olympic ranking points. This was a great opportunity for us to test our abilities and fight against strong opponents.

We arrived in Las Vegas in the afternoon on January 28, 2018. We headed straight to the hotel where the tournament was being held, and after we were settled we went to the convention center where the competition was held to get our credentials from registration. We were very excited and ready to fight.

Teams started arriving with their coaches, and our former master was there too. It felt like our destiny to keep meeting at competitions. He looked frustrated and confused that his plan to destroy us hadn't worked yet. In fact, it was quite the opposite. This was our third year of training on our own without him, and our success was astonishing. Our performance at the recent President's Cup showed everyone, including him, that we don't break easily.

We were alone in the competition, as always. The Olympic coach's team was there too, but they alone hung out together, and ate together — we were kept out of the group. We were used to feeling that kind of isolation from other team members, so we and our parents spent the days at the competition together, all of us trying to avoid our former master and his team.

The Olympic coach's partner had made it very clear the last time we met that their dojo wouldn't be involved in any action against our former master. They wouldn't protect us in public, and they wouldn't defend us if our former master offended us. We understood where they came from. In the end, it wasn't an issue with the sport, but rather, a political game in which the coaches, masters, and teams had a part. There were no rules, no respect, and no limits in this game. We had to find a way to protect ourselves.

Our parents contacted the American Center for Safe Sports to ask for protection from our former master—as no one, including the Olympic coach and his partner, was willing to step in and stop the mental and emotional abuse that was being targeted at us by our former master and his fellow coaches. At the time, Safe Sports issued a temporary restraining order against our former master which stated that he had to stay away from us and not speak to us during the competition. We thought this would give us temporary protection, so that we could move on. But, unfortunately, his authority proved to be above any order.

Jonah won three big fights that day and was ready for the quarter-final, the match that would have put him in the top four. Because of the restraining order, he felt very safe sitting in the waiting area, as our parents sat in the stands opposite the ring where the fight was supposed to take place. Unfortunately, Jonah began not to feel well. He asked the Olympic master to hold the fight for a while, because he needed to visit the restroom, as it was an emergency. They laughed at him because he was such a little kid, but no one knew the story behind his request. Our dad took Jonah, and two minutes later, they both came back. My father was very angry. It turned out that our former master had found his way to Jonah in the holding area and threatened him again. Jonah was subjected to the agonizing experience of terrible, abusive behavior by our former master once again, vomiting in the restroom out of fear. Our father had to help him catch his breath and told him to refuse to fight.

Jonah has always been a stubborn child, never letting go of something he thinks he can do. Jonah's experience in the garage had changed his perception of himself and his strength, but our former master had caused him temporary confusion, as he tried to sow terror in Jonah's heart. But, he hadn't succeeded to shake the power inside Jonah. Our former master's abusive behavior in the holding area made Jonah see the extent of the threat and humiliation our former master felt due to our success. He felt threatened that he would lose his good name, especially when we succeeded after he committed to destroy us. Jonah did not agree with our father and insisted on continuing his fight. There was no longer a fight to earn a medal for Jonah; it was a fight to regain his dignity and respect. He wanted to send a message to the bullies, our former master, his fellow trainees, and anyone else who wanted to use their power to block us that the fear they were spreading would not succeed in stopping us from what we wanted to be or what we had in mind. No one stood with Jonah in the waiting area at that time. He had been alone and no coach or any athlete had the guts to say this was wrong. Who would stand by his side and defend him?

Jonah fought hard while feeling nauseous. He gathered what remained of his inner strength and faced his opponent with honor and courage. Although he did not feel his legs that day, he fought with his heart. Sadly, it wasn't enough, and Jonah lost his battle by just one point. We didn't care that he hadn't won; we were all so proud of him that day, as he did not give into the fear. Jonah continued his fight to show everyone that a young kid's tenacious mentality and inner strength were more powerful than any abusive coach, or even the master's powers.

Jonah sent his clear message that day, and everyone heard it. It was a truly traumatic experience for Jonah, but he refused to surrender himself to the darkness. Jonah refused to let our former master's intentions make him quit his fight—even when he threatened Jonah and tried to abuse him mentally, verbally, and emotionally. While Jonah was disappointed that he couldn't stand on the podium, we all realized how much he had grown mentally that day. Jonah was willing to face his fears and refused to end the fight, deciding that he was the only one with the power to stop himself. He had fought under fear, threat, terror, and abuse and was mentally and emotionally manipulated in front of several coaches claiming to carry the principles of the sport with their titles. It was the day we both decided to move in a different direction.

We couldn't keep wasting our energy fighting negativity and darkness; we had to find our way away from this point. We would need to continue on our own—like we started on our own, with no one to rely on. We will never be held behind. We have our own identities, strengths, and visions, and we will bring the three of them together to create new unstoppable, unbreakable, and unshakable versions of ourselves. We would push ourselves to our limits and leave the darkness behind.

Our story with Safe Sports ended on the day our parents received an e-mail from them, after one year of unreasonable action claiming that, after investigation, they found our former master not guilty and that our parents made up the whole story. We were not surprised by this result. Corruption in the sport was higher than any expectation at the time, not only in Taekwondo, but also in gymnastics and other sports. Two people from the committee investigating our case (one a well-known coach, and the other an athlete from the state federation) were best friends with our former master. It was a closed case from the start. Even with the psychiatrist's report stating the psychological damage done to us as a result of our master's previous abuse, no one believed us or stood by us. We don't know if it was because of our race, religion, or just who we are.

We decided to leave our case, no longer dwelling in the past. We chose to believe that everything would be revealed in time. However, we can't fight corruption, which is like cancer spreading violently through our sport in an ugly and painful way. Racism is a cancer that threatens our health.

CHAPTER TEN
Flowers Bloom in the Night: Prosperity Comes from Healing

Healing is a difficult process that we had to go through to heal. We needed to move forward by changing the environment that attracted negativity to us. For example, living in the dark is unhealthy for our minds and bodies; getting into unnecessary fights wastes our energy and shifts our focus in unwanted directions.

We need a strong will to heal. We must have a purpose to keep us motivated to overcome our obstacles, press forward, and continue to achieve our goals! Feeling pain, feeling wronged, and living in darkness had given purpose to our mission; it kept us thriving and allowed us to achieve success. Sometimes, pain plays a positive role in our development, and without realizing it, we are living with it.

Consistency was critical to our growth, and we needed to keep going—no breaks, no setbacks. We had to take full responsibility for our own development. After what we faced at the US Open, we realized that we were alone on this journey. We must take care of each other, push each other to grow, and focus on our common goal. We took an oath together to reach our destination with our own strength, our own power, and hard work. There were no shortcuts, and no head start. We will dance our own dance, and it will be the best.

Reading was our main and only source for gaining wisdom and insights; we needed to study our sport—from its origin—to go back to the past where it started, and learn Taekwondo from the original people who created this sport. We had to go back in history to drink from the river of knowledge; we must make sure that we understand the principles of Taekwondo. We needed to know our sport in a different way than it had been presented to us. If we wanted to succeed in our mission, we had to restore our love for our sport in a divergent manner, away from the negativity that had accompanied us the past three years. We had to start from the beginning and build a new foundation driven by our values.

We began our reinvigorated study of Taekwondo based on the stories of legends—the values they spread, the way they were trained, how they built their mindset, and what part of the body they focused on when strengthening their abilities. It took us a lot of time to study, research, and apply what we learned in our training. However, we were focused on one core task: strengthening our minds and abilities and making our minds the master of our bodies.

Although the garage was a restrictive venue for us at first, we had learned how to turn our limiting forces into driving forces. We had learned to embrace our skills by entrusting our abilities. Through continuous practice, we improved our learning and memory skills. Through repetitive practice, we strengthened our minds to build lasting capabilities in good times and bad. We were able to stimulate our minds to reach the level where we were able to see our limits and obstacles as opportunities to rise to the challenge.

We worked to expand our abilities through a series of exercises that strained our patience and challenged us to know we had reached our maximum mental strength. The garage gave us the perfect opportunity to test the limits of our minds. We were training under unbelievably challenging circumstances that redirected our thinking, enhanced our reasoning skills, and launched our vision to see beyond.

No matter what skills we possess, what techniques we use, or who's sitting in our chair, we won't conquer our fears and obstacles if we don't have a really strong mindset. The light in the darkness has always lived within us. At that moment, we realized the power of these words:

I am able.

We have always believed in hope; it has been our only friend during the storm; it fed our minds and hearts. Hope breeds motivation, and motivation strengthens the will. When our will became strong, limitations dissolved, colors bloomed, and a bright light shined down in the garage, after dark and stormy nights. Hope had been our candle in the grimmest of times, and hope charged us with the energy that made our hearts beat with passion again.

Our garage training became a permanent state—with no places to go and no team to train with. We had to accept training in our garage and adapt to it, so our garage became a place where we shared our dreams, where we sweated together, where we trained together, and where we laughed together. We spent hours training in the garage, correcting our mistakes, and digging our way through. Finally, the garage became a place of joy, instead of our prison. Our perception of the garage changed daily. We started having fun during breaks; we danced together, sang together, and shared unforgettable memories. Positivity changed our vision and perception of the obstacles and limitations we faced in our garage. We found the solution through adaptation, and this led to finding our inner peace.

Adaptation is Power (Jonah)

One of the most powerful realizations we captured together has been knowing we had the privilege of writing our own story; employing adaptation as a technique for overcoming our limitations, which sprouted positivity within us. We aimed for breakthroughs, learned to set very big, bold (almost unrealistic) goals, and promised to put forth the extraordinary effort necessary to achieve our goals and overcome our limitations. Without a positive attitude, we could not heal and move forward. Training in a box didn't mean that the meager available space limited us. We came to realize that although our bodies were limited by training in a place as small as our garage, our minds were free to soar. We had the freedom to imagine, the freedom to create, and the freedom to inspire ourselves regardless of our surroundings.

Through imagination, we make the impossible possible, work hard at our greatest task—building strong communication skills between our minds and bodies; stimulating our minds to think faster and more efficiently, to weather the storm, adapt to limited space, and produce defense mechanisms that can adapt to our limitations. We created our own workouts to fit the limited space, upgraded our physical training, began to put extra pressure on our minds, and prepared to suffer with joy. We altered our outlook on our situation, and with that, we transformed our results by taking our minds and body to another level we would not have reached without training in the garage. We took an oath together to strengthen ourselves by feeding our minds with positive energy, and we did it together.

Faith is Power

Our mother used to say these words to us all the time: "Always remember that you have the power to write your own story. No one can finish what God started." And she was right. Our belief in God was strong, our belief in our abilities was deep, and our trust in each other was unshakable.

We turned our struggles into strength, challenged that strength, controlled our mindset, and became masters of our destiny, ready to write the next chapter of our journey. Immediately after the U.S. Open, we began communicating with a Taekwondo Federation of a country overseas as both of us hold dual citizenship with this country and America because both of our parents are immigrants who came to the United States in search of opportunity. Our Dad asked the Olympic coach if he could speed up the process because he had many connections, and we knew without those connections no one would listen to us or accept us—because we had tried to contact the federation so many times before and no one responded to our e-mail or calls. Thankfully, the coach pushed the process and spoke to the Federation directly to explain our situation. A few weeks later, we received an e-mail from the country Taekwondo Federation inviting us to try training with one of their country's teams. They quickly provided us with the necessary documents to sign us up at one of the Taekwondo clubs in the country.

Our parents submitted the required papers and the process of changing our WT-GAL, World Taekwondo Global Licence for Athletes began. The Olympic coach loved the idea that both of us would start fighting under the name of another country. It would keep us out of the limelight here in the U.S., while making things easier for him with the other coaches and dojos in the U.S. It appeared as if a heavy weight was lifted off his shoulders when we joined another national team. Now we belonged to another club, another team outside the U.S., and as a result, would be far from any event inside the U.S. Now we could fight internationally, far from home and away from our former master. We felt comfortable being away too, and we were ready to fly.

Our first two international tournaments were the Belgium Open and the Dutch Open. We worked extremely hard leading up to these two tournaments. Although we were not yet ready to fight under the new country flag, because our documents weren't quite complete yet, we were thrilled to embark on this adventure together, and to fight outside the U.S., far away from the negativity and corruption. Unfortunately, financial limitations prevented the Olympic coach from joining us on our trip to Europe, but that didn't stop us.

We traveled to Europe after the Olympic coach talked to one of his friends who agreed to coach us there. It didn't make much difference to us who would be sitting in the chairs near us as we competed. Truthfully, we preferred that no one was in that chair, as the new coach didn't know our capabilities, our strengths, or our weaknesses. He had also traveled with his team to compete in the two openings. He was just doing us a favor when he agreed to be there for us, in name only.

Dutch Open: Eindhoven, March 9-10, 2018 (Sally)

We arrived in Eindhoven in the Netherlands a few days before the opening and went straight to the hotel, as it was the headquarters of the competition. Several national teams started arriving with their coaches, as well as the competition's doctors, and referees. How strange it felt to be in such a high-level environment, surrounded by extremely elite athletes, Olympic coaches, and an exceptionally big competition.

We looked at ourselves, two 12-year-olds from a small garage in the U.S., traversing oceans and continents while carrying big dreams. We experienced many mixed emotions at that moment. We were proud to just be there, trying to spar in a competitive international tournament. Still, at the same time, we were afraid to be in the ring, not because we doubted ourselves, but because we doubted our chances of getting a fair chance. We trained non-stop, changed our vision, studied our bodies, watched and learned about our sport—but we still didn't have what these other athletes had. They had coaches to support them every step of the way. They got the medical care they needed, the nutrients they required, had their check-in process completed for them, their credentials secured. The competitors received the mental and emotional support any athlete would dream of having. We, on the other hand, were alone and responsible for everything. Our parents got us our credentials, fed us, cared for our medical needs, and did their best to make us feel good, but we were missing something crucial: a sense of belonging.

We were supposed to meet the coach who would coach us in the competition for the first time. Unfortunately, he was with his team in a different hotel away from where the competition was supposed to take place. As a result, we didn't have the opportunity to train with him before the competition, or even get the chance to meet him face-to-face. We weren't able to talk to him so he could get to know us better and learn our sparring style in the ring. We felt lonely and the determination inside us started to waiver.

We got up the next day and headed to the hotel conference room where the weight checks would be performed. We lined up with several athletes, mostly seniors and juniors. After hours of waiting and delays, the doors opened but the security officer at the door wouldn't let our mom into the weight room with us. As I was young, my mom tried to convince the security officer that she needed to be with me inside so she could take care of me. However, the officer insisted that my mother not be allowed in, so I ended up going in alone.

Fortunately, a group of athletes from Spain told our mother not to worry as they would make sure I would be okay inside. These girls were so kind and gave me water and some snacks after I weighed in; they kept me with them even though it was just for a few minutes. It felt amazing to receive that kind of support and it was such a kind gesture from this team and these athletes. They showed sportsmanship and discipline. But, it also reminded me of my isolation, the lonely nights of rehearsals, just me and Jonah, and the four walls in our garage.

The next day we headed to the competition, prepared for everything God had planned for us. We accepted our fate of being alone, and we still hadn't had a chance to meet the coach who was supposed to coach us in the tournament. We walked with heavy steps toward the convention center, looking at the teams around us, walking behind their coaches with confidence and strength. Our parents were our only support system and they went beyond their capabilities to motivate us. As usual, our mother was our fundamental source of hope. Our dad had always been there for us, supporting us financially and emotionally. Even though his schedule was busy, he always put us first and never missed a competition or tournament. Aside from ensuring we had a healthy mental and physical environment in the garage, they showered us with their love and embraced us with their warmth.

We entered the convention center with our dream in one hand and our disappointment in the other, not sure which way things would go. On our way, we were stopped by the coach who was supposed to coach us, who was accompanied by his team. He told us he might not be available at the start of the competition to coach us because he had a lot of athletes from his team lining up for their matches. However, his friend and fellow coach from Holland would coach us if he couldn't. This was a painful slap in the face as we were already there on our own, coming from isolation and running away from harsh rejection. We gave up hope at that moment, and this news left us feeling desperate and hopeless.

We took our seats on the floor near the waiting area and waited for our first match to be called. It was early in the morning and we trained together every half hour to warm up before the matches. It was a very long day, and it wasn't until 6 p.m. that Jonah was called for his first match. We started looking for the coach who was supposed to sit in Jonah's chair, but he was coaching one of his players in another ring. Jonah stood in the ring waiting for the coach. As he waited he began to lose his passion and excitement.

We knew we would always be on our own, fighting our battle ourselves. It took a while for the coach's friend to come to the ring after our parents went looking for him. How stressful our experience was and how humiliated we felt at that moment! Finally, the match started, and Jonah started his battle with a discouraged heart. We had worked so hard to prepare for this competition, traveling abroad in search of a fair chance with the hope for once that justice and fairness would prevail. Sadly, we were crushed by the ugly reality that we would always be alone. Jonah fought with an aching heart and lost his first match. We had all lost our confidence and hope at this point. It was a tough day for all of us, and I couldn't stand watching Jonah's dream get crushed by irresponsible behavior toward us. How painful it was to feel that there was no one to support us, to know that we were alone wherever we went.

After the other coach's athletes had lost their matches, the coach came to my ring and was available to coach me, but it was too late. I felt my legs get heavy and my mind filled with misty clouds. Two hours later, I was called up for my first match; I fought carelessly and desperately. There was no reason to keep fighting for a dream that was cruelly shattered by reckless behavior and disrespectful attitudes toward our hard work.

We both lost our first fights that day. We both cried in pain and in deep silence. It wasn't the losses that made us cry, but the agonizing feeling of constant disappointment and the neglect of others toward us. We had just turned 12 years old, but the sadness in our hearts was bigger than us, so big it could cover oceans. The coach apologized for what happened that day and promised that he would be there for us in the next competition the following week in Belgium. We couldn't blame the coach for what happened that day, after all, he had come with his team and they were his priority. But that still didn't lessen the despair we felt.

We closed our chapter on our first international European Championship, burying our disappointments, taking a deep breath, and looking forward to the life that awaited us with a new realization. A new vision that carried hope and positivity for better opportunities ahead. As our mother always told us, it was our destiny to do wonderful things and we were determined to prove her right.

Belgium Open: Lommel, March 18, 2018 (Sally)

There will always be adversity, obstacles, disappointments, failures, as well as ups and downs in our lives. Despite all that, we continue to do our best, trying to conquer our obstacles and overcome the odds.

After the Dutch Open, we headed to Amsterdam for a few days off before the next competition in Lommel, Belgium, where we spent some quiet time with our parents. Unfortunately, we got food poisoning and were sick for three days. We were unable to keep any food or drink down, causing us both to lose a lot of weight because of our sickness. Regardless, we headed to the competition in Lommel and checked into our hotel, a resort not far from where the competition was being held.

After the Dutch Open, we headed to Amsterdam for a few days off before the next competition in Lommel, Belgium

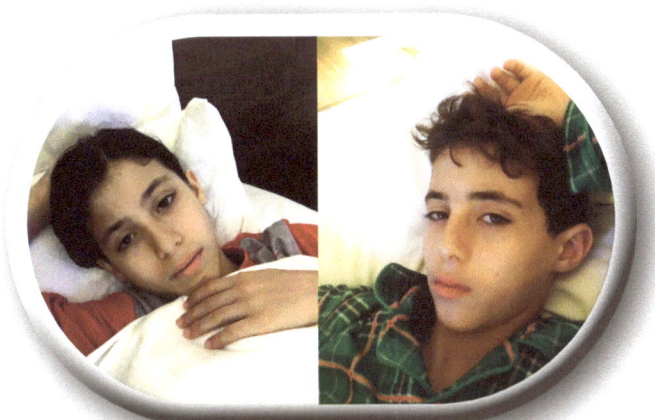

We got food poisoning and were sick for three days. We were unable to keep any food or drink down, causing us both to lose a lot of weight because of our sickness.

Us at the convention center in Lommel, Belgium, where the Belgium Open was held

Practicing together before the beginning of our matches at Belgium Open, Lommel, Belgium

At the Competition hosted resort, Lommel, Belgium

We had to keep up with our schoolwork

The resort had cabins, and while other athletes would exit their cabins and get into waiting cars to go train at the tournament location reserved for them by their federations, we had to walk from our cabin to a nearby shopping center every day to train there in an open space we found. On top of that difficulty, we also had to keep up with our schoolwork. Our middle-school teachers back home believed in us and supported our dreams. They would send us with work while we traveled, so we didn't fall behind. School remained our number one priority, and we had taken full responsibility to keep our grades high and maintain an even balance between school and sport. We believed that our sport and our education complemented each other—we cannot excel in one and fail in the other; we need to excel in both to succeed.

After a few days, we were ready to compete, and that match was enormous. There were many teams and even some well-known Olympic athletes. We were so excited to get into the ring and see what we could do. We met the coach from the Belgium Open again, and this time he was ready to coach us. He was saddened by what happened to us at the Dutch Open because we had traveled so far, flew over the ocean, and paid a lot of money to go and compete in that tournament.

We are getting our credentials

Jonah was the first to begin his fights. He was energetic and happy, and the coach stayed with Jonah most of the time. Jonah felt confident, winning his first three matches while remaining vibrant and full of strength. He was in his quarter-final and had to win four fights to earn a medal. In his fourth match, Jonah was determined to win, fighting a well-known athlete with all his heart. Both of them made it to a sudden death match in which the one who scores first wins. Jonah was careful and patient during the fight. In a move to avoid his opponent's foot, the sensor grabbed Jonah's electronic helmet, and even though it was a no-touch point it gave Jonah's opponent the advantage to win the match.

It was a tough loss, but it had its benefits as well. Jonah had won three matches and had shown what he learned in the garage. Jonah was victorious in his battle over his fear, and against our former master. Jonah triumphed in the battle he was waging with himself—the battle against self-doubt, disappointment, and now knowing his own value. He went from training in a garage alone to fighting and defeating mighty athletes. He had stood firm on one of the stages of international competition, and even though he didn't receive a medal I was very happy for him, as he had shown immense bravery and the courage to fight.

Jonah felt confident, winning his first three matches, while being vibrant and full of strength

Soon after Jonah finished his fights, mine began. It was such a great feeling to be back in the ring; we had missed the ring and sparring with the others. We hadn't been fighting that day to earn medals, but for our love of the sport. Nevertheless, that day I won my three matches and received a bronze medal, my first international European medal, and I was very proud of myself. Although I felt I could win the gold, I knew that my frustration during my fourth match was a result of my losing confidence. I was intimidated by my opponent, a member of the Belgian national team. She was well known in Europe and had the advantage of being surrounded by her coaches and team members. The crowd was all cheering for her, while I was the only one cheering for myself. I made no excuses for my mistakes or setbacks and always took full responsibility for my failures, but that moment shook my confidence. That day I learned an important lesson: if I wanted to win, I had to shut my ears to outside noise, close my eyes so as not to go blind from the bright lights, and only focus on one thing—winning. I learned that the moment I lose my confidence, will be the moment I would lose my battle.

After that day, we came home believing in a new vision of ourselves. We knew we could do it, and that we must do it. We saw ourselves clearly and witnessed the birth of our unbreakable spirits. Despite our hardships and adversities, we had shown courage. We had fought our battles bravely and we were fully capable of standing on our own.

We returned home from our European journey and went straight back to school where we discovered we were way ahead of our peers in all subjects. We had worked hard to meet our teachers' high expectations of us and to show them that we valued the trust they showed us when they allowed us to be absent from school for extended periods. We were at our academic peak and had straight A's in every subject, so we were inducted into the National Elementary Honor Society.

We returned to the garage as well. But our perception of our garage had changed. We now embraced the walls that we previously viewed as limits, and through our limitations in the garage, we learned how to get stronger. Without these walls, we would not have had the strength to insist on achievement. These walls strengthened our minds and challenged us to face our fears, stand firm, and fight for our identities. Without having been forced to train alone in our garage, we wouldn't be who we are now. We wouldn't have been able to break the chains that bound us so that we could grow strong wings to fly. Without our pain, we could not heal, and without our garage, we would not have found ourselves in a position to realize we must put our trust and faith in God. Most importantly, without the suffering we experienced during garage training, we couldn't have learned how to move forward and never give up.

After Belgium, we continued our training in the garage on our own—but this time we were training with joy. Now, in our garage we saw the warmth of our home, and it no longer felt dark and cold. Our mom continued to sit with us, taking videos of our training sessions and nourishing our minds and hearts with her magical words of inspiration that kept us fighting for our dream. She showed us all the videos she had taken since we started training in our garage to prove to us just how much we had grown and improved.

These videos motivated us to go the extra mile to improve. But, even more than our willingness to work hard to continually do better, we needed to continue our mission. Our mom told us stories about many heroes who overcame obstacles, defeated their limitations and achieved their goals. She implanted hope in our hearts and formed a wonderful dream inside our minds. Mom had a great way of lighting the fire within us. Although she was not a physical part of our training, nor did she even give us any feedback on our training methods, mom was our remarkable mental coach, our magnificent life coach. She was our teacher who fed us with positivity and hope. She was the confident, optimistic spirit in the garage, who added a pleasant feeling to our garage training. Our mother was our friend, our teacher, our spiritual mentor, and above all, our loving mom. She repeatedly sacrificed her happiness for ours, staying with us every minute and attending every event. She breathed for us and she believed in us when no one else did.

Our mother's name is Areeg, and she is known as the woman who spreads positivity to those around her. She is kind-hearted mother. Our mom learned from her mother that life requires patience and courage, and she taught those lessons to us. She allowed us to live a life full of joy and happiness without ever mentioning what she wanted or desired for herself. As a family, we loved taking advice and learning life lessons from her. We were always happy when we saw her turn toward us. She had mastered the art of making people feel hopeful and constructive—and if they weren't, she would teach them how to be.

Our mom is a beautiful woman, like an angel. We feel safe when we look at her; her smile makes the room glow with positivity and hope; her laughter can break any form of negativity. She always prayed for us and for others to live happy, peaceful, and blessed lives. She is close to God, trusts Him, and regularly shows her gratitude for what she has, which sets her apart from others. Most people only care about themselves and less about others, but that is not her. She is a selfless, honest, and loving person.

Jonah was the first to begin his fights — He was energetic and happy

I won my three matches and received a bronze medal—
My first international European medal, and I was very proud of myself. Belgium, Lommel

Kindness is Power (Jonah)

Two months after our European tour, the Olympic coach hosted a big training camp. He invited us to take part, even though we had not participated in any training camps in the United States for a long time. To avoid unnecessary negativity, we wanted to go to this specific camp, not for training but to meet someone we had respected and adored since we were little.

The camp invited Mr. Aaron Cook, Olympic Champion, and Ms. Bianca Walkden, Rio 2016, Olympic Bronze Champion. We had known Mr. Cook for a long time, having met him for the first time when we were about seven years old at our former master's dojo when he hosted a training camp there. Mr. Cook was kind, had a big smile, and was down to earth; even though we were young, he treated us with respect and was so kind to us. He even invited us to have a sparring match with him. We were treated like champions by this Olympic champion.

Jonah sparring with Mr. Aaron Cook The Olympic Athlete, when we were about seven years old at our former Master's dojo

Mr. Cook wanted to show us that we were strong enough to stand up to him and compete with him. During that time, we had a strange feeling about him: we felt that he was like an older brother. He was very close to our hearts, and we loved him so much. In 2015, we met Mr. Cook again during a competition in Portland, USA, and even though this interaction lasted only a few minutes, we got the same supportive, encouraging feeling. He was unlike any other athlete we had seen or met. During our European Tour in 2018, we met Mr. Cook once again at the Dutch Open. He was standing in the waiting area about to go into the ring. Despite all the tension, he saw fit to give us a few minutes of his time, as he immediately remembered us. Once again, that feeling of warmhearted familiarity came back. He was a true gentleman and a wonderful person to be around. The respect he showed others set him apart from the rest of the athletes we had met before. We admired him for his positivity, honor, and discipline.

On May 26, 2018, we headed to the Olympic dojo after waking up early. Our hearts were beating rapidly, as we recognized we wouldn't feel comfortable being in the dojo—because of the many coaches and athletes there that we knew didn't like us.

Jonah and I with Mr. Aaron Cook at our former coach Dojo

After the Olympic coach and his former partner broke up due to the many problems his ex-partner had faced, the Olympic coach had to take full responsibility for the big dojo. However, he struggled to keep the dojo running. He got into significant financial difficulty, so our dad had to step in and donate a large amount of money to enable the dojo to remain open. Our father came from a culture that believed in giving without waiting for a reward. He could not see the Olympic coach face a financial crisis without stepping in to help him. Along those lines, our dad even continued to pay tuition, although we didn't practice in the dojo or train with the coach over Zoom. Soon, the Olympic coach got a new partner, one of our former master's friends, who was one of the state coaches. Unfortunately, that new partner had been poisoned not to like us thanks to the rumors he heard from our former master.

We walked into the dojo with trepidation and doubt. We always try to avoid or walk away from negative people. However, the moment we entered the dojo we noticed the Olympic coach's new partner. On our way to see Mr. Cook, we cautiously passed several coaches who were allies of our former master. We tried to ignore their baffling games as we headed to the table where Mr. Cook was signing autographs with Mrs. Walkden, a double Olympic medalist.

Mr. Cook saw us from afar, put down the pen he was holding, and stood confidently while smiling at us. His reaction made us feel self-assured, so we greeted him with handshakes and hugs. We will never forget that moment— he was an Olympic athlete and we were just 13-year-olds. Still, the respect he showed us was indicative of the unique person he is. He introduced us to Mrs. Walkden and told her of our story of training alone in the garage.

In 2015, we met Mr. Aaron Cook again during a competition in Portland, USA

May, 2018, at the Olympic Coach's dojo

May, 2018, at the Olympic Coach's dojo

During our European Tour in 2018, we met Mr. Aaron Cook once again at the Dutch Open. He was standing in the waiting area about to go into the ring and despite all the tension, he felt he gave us a few minutes of his time as he immediately remembered us

Sally with Mr. Aaron Cook at Dutch Open

His generosity and kindness at that moment caused our world to change. The darkness, fear, doubt, and disappointment we had lived with the past years faded in a moment. The positivity of this Olympic athlete revealed the true values of our sport. He held the essence, spirit, respect, and discipline of Taekwondo in his heart. Through Mr. Cook, we felt the power of our sport. Although the interaction lasted only a few minutes, it cemented our determination to keep going. Moreover, his supportive inspiration heightened our love for our sport. We knew that God had put Mr. Aaron Cook on our path to tell us not to give up; to keep fighting for our identities, dreams, goals, and principles and to continue the battle for the love of our sport. That day was one of the most memorable days of our lives. Our experience with Mr. Cook, albeit brief, left a noticeable impact on us both. In addition, Mrs. Walkden showed us respect and encouraged us throughout the boot camp. It was exactly what we needed.

Although none of the coaches there, including the Olympic coach's associates, liked what they saw in us, our confidence and positivity were not affected by their negative reactions. We continued training alone in our garage after that day and continued our journey toward achieving our goal. Mr. Cook's generous gesture charged us with positive energy and boosted our confidence. This was a face we had unfortunately never seen in our sport—the face of true sportsmanship. Since that day, our respect and love for Mr. Cook grew even stronger.

A new chapter of a new journey had begun. We were officially members of the new country's national team. It was an arduous journey as we were living in the U.S., training in our garage alone, and the new country's national team trained in their country at the national team headquarters. It was as if it was our destiny to be left on our own, but we were determined to take full responsibility for the trust given to us by the new country's national coaches and the new club we joined. The next international tournament would be our way of saying "thank you" to the new country's Taekwondo Federation, and we knew we must represent them well.

European Cadet Championship Qualification Plovdiv, 2018 (Sally)

After the training camp at the Olympic coach's dojo, we traveled to Bulgaria for our third international competition, our first tournament competing under another country's name. It was official. We were fighting for another country. This was the best solution for the Olympic coach, as now he didn't have to worry about us. We were basically not part of his team. We would not attend any competitions within the U.S., and, most importantly, he would still have the chance to travel the world with us for free.

After the training camp at the Olympic coach dojo, we traveled to Bulgaria for our third international tournament and our first tournament competing under another country's name.

The Olympic coach asked our father if he wanted him to accompany us to the international competitions. This arrangement had benefits for us both: Accompanying us would ensure that the coach did not miss the international stage, especially after he left his job as national coach for a foreign country; we would benefit from the coach's deep connections to the sport and the protection he offered us from our former master. We couldn't refuse the Olympic coach's offer because we knew the depth of his connections in the sport, and how dangerous and long the reach of our former master remained. Without the coach's protection, our former master could easily wipe us off the Taekwondo map. That is the ugly face of our sport: the existence of corruption. Many athletes had been crushed by the cruel feet of many coaches because they dared question, criticize, or fight bullies and abuse. We were not going to give our former master the chance to crush us. We remained focused on our ultimate goal that went beyond our sport and medals. The mission that no one knew about.

Our father bought a ticket for the Olympic coach to join us on our trip to Bulgaria. He booked him a hotel room and gave him a generous coaching fee. Our family was annoyed, but knew we had no choice. He used us because he knew we had to obey him or else he could use his power to make us disappear. Should an irreconcilable dispute arise, the disagreement would suddenly be reduced to the word of an Olympic coach with a long legacy, against us, the words of troublemakers training alone in their garage.

We arrived in Bulgaria, rented a car, and drove to Plovdiv,
a lovely and ancient city, located in southern Bulgaria

Jonah and I at Plovdiv, touring the city

For the first three days of our trip, we were alone as the Olympic coach hadn't arrived yet. Therefore, we had to train alone, as always — at the hotel gym, Plovdiv, Bulgaria

The next morning, we got up, ready for our competition, and headed to the convention center. It was the qualifying championship for the European Cadet Championship and we were very determined to win

We arrived in Bulgaria, rented a car, and drove to Plovdiv, a lovely and ancient city located in country's southern region. We were on our own for the first three days of our trip, as the Olympic coach hadn't arrived yet. Therefore, we had to train alone, as always, and work on making weight. Our mother was with us, as usual, sitting on the hotel gym floor, cheering us up and cheering us on, mom continued taking pictures and videos of our training sessions. Making memories together was some of the most unforgettable and happiest of moments that we created together—during our travels, training in the garage, and during competitions.

Our mother was careful to document these moments so we could see how we started together and everything we achieved. She ensured that we grew together in a very healthy and loving environment. Mom was always with us and always nurtured a close and warm relationship between us. We are fraternal twins, but it has always felt like we were one soul in two separate bodies. We complete each other and we have a unique relationship that makes others wonder how we became so close. We are best friends, siblings, and partners. We never argue with each other or cause each other pain.

Our mother instilled profound love in our hearts. She raised us on essential principles, values, and morals, and always told us to see God in everything we do and every word we say. Mom emphasized God's love in our hearts and magnified His blessings and grace. We were close to God, so we always tried to act as He commanded us.

Our father was also always there for us. He worked from the hotel during the days, and we all spent the evenings together. Dad was willing to risk his work not to have to leave us alone. He never missed any of our competitions, paid a lot of money to cover our competition and travel expenses, steadfastly believed in us, and followed us wherever we competed.

We had both been in the hotel gym with our mom, working on losing weight—it was the last pound I needed to lose. Jonah's body was different from mine, and he was ready for the next day. I've had hypothyroidism since I was three, and I gained weight fast. My body refused to cooperate with me to get the weight down. One of the biggest hurdles I had to overcome was staying healthy and watching my diet. Our mother always refused to let us starve ourselves to lose weight during competitions, like many athletes do in martial art sports. She always helped us remain in good shape and nourished us with healthy food. Therefore, the only way I could lose my remaining weight was to exercise. Running wasn't my favorite thing, but I had to do it if I wanted to keep my body healthy and control my weight. I am not a fan of exercising on machines at gyms, as I prefer to be in nature, running outside, and training with Jonah in the great outdoors. Having been trained in a garage, I developed a discomfort with small, dark places. I didn't like going to the gym and preferred training with Jonah outside, on the track field, or at the park.

The hotel gym made me nauseous, and I couldn't stay there. I wanted to run outside on the city street, but I couldn't because I couldn't run alone in a strange city. Jonah was tired, and he needed to save his energy for the competition. Our mother was willing to do anything to make us feel happy and comfortable. But, of course, our mental health was our priority. After she saw me struggle to make weight in the cramped hotel gym, she suggested we go for a run outside together, although she wasn't used to running or training due to a health issue in her lower back as a result of a car accident. Still, she insisted on running with me and told me that she would feel more comfortable if she helped me lose the remaining weight that I had left. I couldn't refuse. I wanted to lose weight and get a long night's sleep, even though I was extremely tired from the process. Despite my exhaustion, we went on a quick run through the city streets. My mother smiled at me the whole time and cheered me on, despite the fact I knew that every step she took while running caused her terrible pain. Our mother ate the same foods we ate while cutting weight, in the same portions. She was living the same life we lived as athletes to support and motivate us. She never gave up and coached us not to give up on ourselves. She taught us to love challenging ourselves, stand firm, fight honorably and proudly for the right things, and stick to what we think is right. She understood that the most important thing to train in an athlete was their mind. She fed our minds with positivity, strength, power, and determination.

We returned to the hotel after our run. Our father was finishing up work and Jonah was resting in the room, trying to recover from the long travel, weight cut, and endless hours of training we completed before arriving in Bulgaria. We tried to sleep that night to get ready for the next day, but we couldn't. Instead, we stayed up all night, praying to God to bring peace and calm to our hearts and minds, to keep us safe, and to grant us a good day.

After arriving in Bulgaria the night before, the Olympic coach met us in the lobby the next morning. We drove to the convention center together to get our credentials and weigh in. The meeting with him was cold, as his mind seemed to be somewhere else. It was clear that he came to Bulgaria for another reason than coaching us. Still, we tried to ignore these feelings in the hope of getting a better opportunity to train this time. We had longed to see a coach in our chair and thought he was there for us, but we realized the painful truth too late.

After hours of waiting in line, we got our credentials and made the desired weight for our divisions. Next, the Olympic coach met up with other coaches while we went to eat and get ready for the competition the next day. We were exhausted from the long day and very much needed to rest. However, later that evening, around 9 PM, the Olympic coach called our father and told him he wanted us to go to the gym so he could work with us on some kicks. Our father told him we were tired and needed to sleep. The Olympic coach insisted that he had to train us even though it was getting late and so we couldn't refuse him, as he had the power and authority and we had to respect him. So, we met him in the gym for a truly unnecessary and very light training session. We realized that he met with us just so that he could say that he had trained and prepared us before the next day's competition. It was just a show for him and we ended up going to bed late that night in a bad mood.

The next morning, we got up and headed to the convention center, ready for our competition. It was the qualifying championship for the European Cadet Championship and we were very determined to win.

Jonah was excited, happy, and ready to fight. However, the minute he entered the ring his face changed, and felt as if he had already lost. The change in his face reminded us of when he was younger and still being trained by our former master. During that time, our former master sent Jonah into the ring with fear and doubts. He would constantly threaten him and warn him not to lose his fights, yelling at him a lot. And, when Jonah lost a match, our former master would leave the ring in a rage leaving Jonah still standing alone at the ring, overcome with grief.

Jonah loved Taekwondo and every minute of training, but he hated being in the ring and fighting. He suffered a lot mentally and emotionally in the ring because of our former master and had not yet recovered. After our former master left us, our parents discovered that Jonah and I had been traumatized by fear and years of mental and emotional abuse at his hands. They took both of us to a trauma specialist and after we had several sessions at her clinic. She concluded that we met the DSM-V diagnostic criteria for chronic Post-Traumatic Stress Disorder (PTSD) (F43.12).

We both had traumatic experiences that left us living with anxiety, panic attacks, fear, and consistent nights filled with nightmares. We couldn't recover, so we refused to return to the doctor's office to continue treatment. Going there and continuing to talk about the issue made us even sadder. Therefore, our parents decided to stop the treatment after we asked them to do so. Our parents always respected us and trusted our courage. We saw our path to recovery and healing in our garage training—and the more we trained, the more fully we continued to recover and heal. Setting a goal helped us focus on something positive and closed many doors filled with darkness. However, it didn't cure our fear of being in the ring. When we were fighting under the name of our former master, we were fighting for him and fighting out of fear. The fear of losing, the fear of becoming the next victim of his verbal and emotional abuse, afraid he would shame us if we lost our match, or call us stupid, or losers. Conversely, if we won, our former master would take credit for our victories and tell everyone it was because of him that we won.

Jonah lost his first match that day and did not try to fight. Instead, Jonah was desperate, disappointed, and sad. A complex struggle emerged within him. It was a struggle between his commitment to the sport he loved and his rejection of the repeated traumatic experiences he faced within the sport. He cried a lot that day, in pain and despair. Jonah wanted to win so badly. He wanted to overcome the obstacles we faced together in our garage, and wanted us to heal once and for all.

The Olympic coach did not help Jonah, but started blaming him for his loss, raising his voice intensely to tell Jonah that he lost because he did not listen to the coach. At that moment, the Olympic coach added more shame and sadness to Jonah. Our mother could not stand watching Jonah being insulted by the coach and had to stand up once again to protect Jonah's mental health and self-confidence.

Our mother politely reminded the Olympic coach what it means to have a supportive coach next to their athlete, especially after a heavy loss. She told the coach that he should be a positive light for Jonah at that moment. Jonah needed his support and encouragement, not his blame. Our mother asked the coach to stop blaming Jonah for the loss, especially when he was aware of Jonah's painful story with our former coach.

The Olympic coach put a fake smile on his face to hide his negative feelings for our mother and nodded his head in agreement. However, he never forgot how she spoke to him. That day marked the beginning of a different treatment of our mother by the Olympic coach. He changed his behavior toward her and started throwing random words at her in a very sarcastic tone, contending that she was "training" us and that she was acting like a "professional." These were familiar, recurring phrases we had heard before from our former master when my mother asked him to stop his abusive behavior toward us.

On that day, I could not stand seeing Jonah so humiliated. He is very talented, passionate, and loves our sport. Jonah deserves better chances to prove himself. He deserves to have someone who believes in his abilities in his chair. Unfortunately, the Olympic coach did not reflect any positive energy that would motivate Jonah, and his negative attitude toward Jonah—from the beginning—made Jonah doubt his abilities.

We knew the Olympic coach had not come to the competition to coach us, but rather to keep his connections alive with the other coaches all over the world. He was just using us to cover his international travel expenses and keep his contacts and lines of communication within the international Taekwondo industry alive.

I decided to focus on my upcoming competition and concentrate on winning for both myself and Jonah. To do so I would have to block my ears from hearing any words coming from the Olympic coach and focus my eyes on the goal: the European qualification championship.

My first match was a huge success. I was fighting for Jonah and remembering every person who had rejected us, every obstacle we faced together, and every painful minute we lived together in the garage. I fought for our freedom and our dreams. That day, I didn't feel someone sitting in my chair. My eyes were focused on my mission, my ears were hearing our kicks echo in the garage, and my heart was beating faster than any previous time. I wanted to race through that moment and beat our sadness, disappointments, fears, and pain. I wanted to open my broken wings and fly up to the sky, where I could see our obstacles fade away and our pain too. I fought hard enough to earn my qualification for the

European Cadet Championship and showed everyone who caused us pain that we would never give up.

My eyes were focused on my mission, my ears were hearing our kicks echo in the garage, and my heart was beating faster than the existing time. I wanted to race that moment and beat our sadness, disappointments, fears, and pain. I wanted to open my broken wings and fly up to the sky where I could see our obstacles fade away and our pain too

I fought hard enough to earn my qualification for the European Cadet Championship and showed everyone who caused us pain that we would never give up

The Olympic coach was happy, thinking he was the one who made me win, telling Jonah that I had won the championship because I had listened to his advice. I ignored him and instead focused on Jonah at that moment. Jonah was not just my twin brother, he was my partner and my only friend. It was Jonah who had helped me improve my techniques over the past years. It was Jonah who was focused on strengthening me, so much so that he would let me kick him as hard as I could so that I could know my strength and improve my skills. He let me practice on him even though I was no physical help to him, due to my smaller size. He didn't care, though. Always a gentleman, and never wanting to hurt me, he continued to help me while he worked alone on the dummy that we had in our garage to improve his fighting techniques and practice sparring.

After the competition, the Olympic coach headed back to the U.S. and our family flew to the new country to meet the head coach of the national team. He wanted us to meet the national coaches and the national team and have a team trial during a training camp with them, so they could have the opportunity to get to know us better, since we lived so far away.

Our parents' relatives live in the new country we fight for now, so we were excited to spend some family time with them before the training camp and team trial with the national team—especially since we don't have any relatives back home in the U.S. After some much-needed rest and relaxation with our relatives, we headed to one of the biggest cities in that country to start the training camp with the national team.

The team was very welcoming. We introduced ourselves to the team members, and they asked us why we changed our citizenship and why we wanted to fight under the country name. We were completely honest with the team and told them our story in detail. We believed that they needed to know our story so that they can have a greater understanding of where we came from and what we had been through. Fortunately, they were very friendly, sympathetic, positive, and motivating, and we had a good training with them.

The head coach of the national team at the time was mostly quiet and took his job very seriously, which was the thing we loved most about him, since the first time we met him. He was kind in his conversations with us, and he asked two senior athletes, who were also siblings, to stay with us and help us during training. The head coach spoke in foreign language the whole time, which was difficult for us, since we didn't speak or understand that language. We appreciated that the two sibling brothers translated for us so that we could understood. They explained each exercise to us and helped us a lot with our training. Fortunately, they knew English very well, since they were born in South Africa before moving to the country with their family.

We had a good two weeks of training with the national team. Before we left we were able to say goodbye to everyone and thank them, especially the two brothers for their kindness and help. The coach talked to us about the plans with the team and what the next steps should be going forward. It was a long conversation, but at the end he told us that the national team coaches had decided to send Jonah along with me to the European Cadet Championship in 2018 in Spain, because they watched him during the training camp and liked how he fought. This was the best news for both of us, and Jonah was so excited. Jonah promised the team that he would do everything in his power to bring honor to the team and our club. We head back to the U.S. with a positive attitude, along with many goals to achieve. Our experience with the new country national team was positive and filled our hearts with hope. It was a dream come true.

After our return to the United States, we were surprised to see our photos on the Olympic coach's team's social media page, where they congratulated us on qualifying for the European Cadet Championship. How ironic this behavior was, as the same team had previously refused our parents' request to protect us a year earlier when we were still fighting for the U.S.; during a time when we sorely needed their protection. Now here they were congratulating us as elite international athletes and members of a new country's national team. They want to promote their dojo and say that they have international athletes as members of their team. This move showed true hypocrisy within our sport.

The Olympic coach's old dojo was huge and had a large monthly rent. It was beyond the Olympic coach's ability to pay for it so he moved to a smaller dojo with his new partner. Our father helped the Olympic coach a lot financially, and we opened our house to him and his family. Our father had even helped physically moved the dojo's equipment to their new location, renting a truck and driving for hours to help pack, unpack, and set up the new space. Our dad always had a kind heart and was very generous. We thought this gesture would be appreciated by the coach and his new partner, but we were mistaken. In a matter of months, their real faces were revealed.

The coach's new partner was part of the State coaching team and was on good terms with our former master. Our story of rejection and racism came to light again, but this time it was different. The partner of the Olympic coach started a cold war against us. He ignored us and showed us no respect. He was always trying to humiliate us, especially through his ignorance of us. He had already formed his opinion about our family and us. Our story of our former master traveled with us everywhere we went, as if a ghost was chasing us. People don't realize just how powerful and hurtful stereotypes and prejudices can be. We were victims of the small-minded, racist coaches and their unfair perceptions of us.

Training together with positive attitude at the garage to prepare for The European Championship

Training together at the garage

Garage Training, before The European Championship

Jonah working on his flexibility at the garage to prepare for the European Championship

European Cadet Championship: December 5, 2018, Spain

How amazing it was to see the way positivity motivated, inspired, and strengthened us after we visited the new country and met with the national team. Despite the negativity we faced at the hands of our new coach's partner, we continued to move forward and strive for more. As a result, we were able to vanquish the darkness and conquer our limitations. We were able to navigate an ocean of opportunity that allowed us to discover new paths free from pessimism and pain. Despite all the limitations we had in our garage, and regardless of the four walls that reminded us daily of our isolation, we had a mission—we were training alone in the garage to our full potential.

Qualification for the European Cadet Championship altered our perception of our capabilities. We managed to make our way forward with our own hands. We had defeated the obstacles put in place by our former master, after he swore that he would destroy us. We wished we had the chance to stand in front of him now, look him in the eye, and tell him that we had already gone far and beyond his expectations. Despite him and his devious, antagonistic efforts, we arrived at our destination because of hard work, determination, and a strong mentality. We had no one to count on, and no one to pave the way for us. We wanted to tell him how grateful we were to him for driving us to realize our potential. When he decided to seclude us in our garage, we realized it was our deep faith in God that enabled us to trust our abilities. We wanted to tell him that God's plans were greater than his.

After we returned from Europe, our mother suggested that we might need to change our training style during our sparring sessions together, so that we were more aggressive with one another. She told us no one would be nice to us in the ring and that had to raise our training level to be more realistic to ensure we would not be surprised during a competition, as had just happened to Jonah. As usual, we continued our daily night training in our garage. At that time, we had just started our second year of middle school. We would go to school early, work extra hard on our schoolwork, stay after school for volunteer hours, come home to do homework, and then train in the evening.

School continued to be our top priority. Education is the best weapon we can use to overcome life's hurdles. We knew that knowledge was the light we could employ to see our way clearly; it would help us avoid mistakes and find solutions to the obstacles we faced in our garage. So, we focused on elevating our academic performance, developing our training techniques, and helping our community grow. We started to engage in many community service activities, such as: fighting hunger in our community by helping with food drives, organizing clothing drives for children suffering because of domestic violence, and tutoring underprivileged students. We believed that tapping into our humanity would help us to develop and succeed. Helping others and cultivating hope in them had an impact on us, too. We started to feel hopeful again; empowering others had given our life purpose. We began to see ourselves outside of our sport, how we could help others to reach the same level of self-satisfaction we felt—and how we could help our peers discover their abilities just as we did.

Jonah and I at the convention center getting our credential/Marina d'Or, Spain

We are at the holding area during the European Championship, waiting to be called to compete

On November 26, 2018, we set off on our journey to the European Cadet Championship, embracing a dream that had lived in our hearts since we were ten years old. We were flying with our mighty wings, the ones we had grown in our garage where we dreamed together. The competition was in Marina d'Or in Castellón, Spain, where we would meet the new country national team, but our first stop would be Madrid. The Olympic coach also wanted to coach us there, so we bought his tickets, booked his hotel room, and gave him a generous coaching fee.

We met the national team at the hotel in Marina d'Or and joined them in every activity they did. We ate together and trained together. It was nice to have a team and feel welcomed by teammates and coaches. However, Jonah refused to have the Olympic coach with him in the tournament. He did not feel comfortable around him, especially after the humiliating way the Olympic coach treated him during the qualifying tournament in Bulgaria. Jonah told our parents that he wished that the new country coaches could sit in his chair. Still, we couldn't do it. We couldn't turn down the Olympic coach, as we had enough enemies and problems and couldn't risk any more negativity. We had to come to terms with ourselves and accept what we had. We needed to be patient and never open the gates of darkness again. Telling the Olympic coach that we didn't want him to coach us any more would open a door of pain that we are not prepared to endure, as his connections were much stronger than ours. Unfortunately, this fact left Jonah unfocused during our training. He could not get the thought of the Olympic coach's scolding out of his head.

The European Championship ended with me being in fifth place and nothing for Jonah. Poor Jonah; what a treasure of talent, but unfortunately, no coach had been able to find the right key to unlock this treasure. Jonah needed motivation; he needed a coach to believe in him, look him in the eye, and tell him, "Don't worry, I'm here for you, and I believe in you." Jonah needed a coach to bring his athletic fighting spirit back to life. He needed to see that the coach sitting in his chair believed in him. Unfortunately, I was more pragmatic than Jonah. I learned I had to fight on my own, no matter who was sitting in my seat. Jonah lived in a world of values, principles, and morals and was more susceptible to harm.

Although the results of the European Championship were unsatisfactory, we had the privilege of being part of an unforgettable experience. We were so proud of ourselves; we were two kids who trained in a garage and could work hard and move mountains to find our own way. We tasted the sweetness of our victory after we overcame our obstacles. This victory showed who we really were to all the dojos and the coaches who had treated us poorly. We proved that we could overcome our obstacles and conquer our fears. We reached far, and we flew high.

Our goal had become crystal clear to us: medals were not the destination, the podium was not the goal, and giving us a ranking number would not reflect our capabilities. Doing our best, overcoming obstacles, working hard on our own, and standing up for what we believed was what truly mattered.

Jonah and me at the European Championship

Never was the benefit of our positive mindset more clear than during the Covid-19 pandemic, which began in March 2020. While many high-ranking athletes, dojo, coaches, and even Olympic athletes in our sport faced tough times training by themselves inside their homes or their garages for a few weeks, we had years of experience doing so. While they struggled mentally to face the challenges they had to overcome due to these less than ideal circumstances, we were used to such isolation. We were just middle-schoolers, but we were far better equipped to handle this burdensome worldwide situation than they were.

Jonah and me after the European Championship talking to our inner self

CHAPTER ELEVEN
Mentality is the Key: The Light at the End of the Tunnel

2019 was the last year for our Taekwondo journey as cadets and our last chance to qualify for the World Cadet Championship, a dream we wanted desperately to achieve. When we were just 10 years old, we made a promise to ourselves to strive to achieve two crucial goals. The first one was to join the AAU/USA national team, and the second was to go to the World Cadet Championships. We first voiced these dreams in our black belt ceremony speeches, during which the team members began to laugh as they didn't think we would ever reach our goals. No one believed in us and no one supported us back then. Many stood in our way, and many tried to shake our core. We struggled so hard, but we believed in God's power and in the dream He planted in our hearts. The power within us awakened us and ignited the fire within us. We believed in our message, our purpose, and our dream. We had faith in God, and we trusted Him blindly.

We voiced our dreams in our black belt ceremony speeches, during which the team members began to laugh, as they didn't think we would ever reach our goals — Sally delivers her black belt speech

Jonah at our Black Belt ceremony, voicing our dreams to join the AAU/USA National team and to make it to the World Cadet Championship

Black Belt Ceremony

We are getting our black belt and certificates

Here we were in 2019. After nearly four years of anticipation and counting our blessings, we'd joined the AAU/USA national team, traveled beyond the horizon, and had many international achievements. On one hand, we both qualified for the European Cadet Championship, and both earned medals in prestigious tournaments, such as the Canadian Open, the US Open, and the President's Cup. However, on the other hand, we both had gone through painful years of being isolated in our garage, training on our own. We were turned down by several coaches and were betrayed by others. Still, despite all the obstacles and limitations we faced, we kept our dreams alive, making our way forward while our hearts bled from sadness, disappointment, rejection, fear, and terrible pain.

Proving that our limitations did not define us, that our obstacles did not paralyze our creativity. We researched, learned, and charted the vision for our path to success. We were realistic about our expectations of ourselves. We knew the kind of abilities we had, faced our pain and healed ourselves. We bore our scars with honor and pride, and had the privilege to say we wrote our untold story.

After the European Cadet Championships, we returned to the U.S., to our garage, where we began our journey into the unknown together. We went back to the lab where we developed and nurtured our mental strength. We continued our daily practice in the garage. In theory, we were supposed to take a break from training over the weekend to recover from a long and hard week of studying and exercise, but we thought we could use that time to work more effectively on advanced training that we had not been able to do in the garage because of the limited space. So, we decided to transfer our advanced training outside of the garage.

**We decided to transfer our advanced training outside of the garage —
Our high school track opened to the public over the weekend**

Our high school track opened to the public over the weekend, and we saw this as a great opportunity to work on strengthening our core strength, speed, and power. We focused on increasing our speed by doing running sessions, strength exercises, sprint exercises, and blast exercises. We spent over three hours a day training on the track. Practicing outside of the garage changed our moods and cleared our minds. Nature was our second gym. We loved training out in nature and felt free from our limitations, especially when running in the rain.

The Olympic coach began to change his treatment of us and develop a close relationship with our father again. We were a winning ticket to him; a ticket to the outside world. He pretended to be our friend, and we fell for his game. He started to send us weekly text messages asking about our training and if we wanted to come to his dojo. He started visiting us with his family at our house on weekends. Unfortunately, we fell for these friendly gestures. We trusted him and believed he had changed. However, we didn't want to train with him—and we didn't want to go to his dojo either. He kept texting us, telling us he missed us and asked for us to train with him. He wanted us to come to his dojo to help his athletes spar, and he would give us private lessons.

Sally and I work on increasing our speed by doing running sessions, strength exercises, sprint exercises, and blast exercises

Jonah is working on strengthening hand muscles and body

Sally and I doing physical activities at the high school track, Activities outside of the garage changed our moods and cleared our minds — Nature was our gym

Sally doing some resistance training to increase the strength of the legs

Jonah is working on his speed and resistance at the same time

We still paid the monthly tuition fee to the Olympic coaches dojo. Our dad didn't want to stop the payments, because he wanted to help the coach with his financial struggles. Eventually, after the Olympic coach put a lot of pressure on us, we agreed to give Zoom training another chance. It was important to him to ensure we remained in touch with him so that he could continue traveling with us to our international tournaments.

Me and Jonah after the European Cadet Championships, Working on our home garage, where we began our journey into the unknown together. Our lab, where we developed our mental strength

Sally working on her kicks and resistance power

Unfortunately, it only took a few sessions to realize how stressful the Zoom training was, especially when the coach's partner repeatedly pretended that he had forgotten to turn on the camera during training. When he did turn the camera on, it was pointed in a direction that prevented us from seeing the training clearly—despite the number of times we told the Olympic coach *and* his partner that we could not adequately view the training to productively participate — and furthermore, we could not train in this stressful environment, especially since we were already training in a highly stressful situation in our garage. The partner attempted to ignore us in every possible way. It was yet another painful experience to go through.

Our parents talked to the Olympic coach about this issue. The new partner claimed that our parents were too involved in our training and needed to step back. It was a hopeless case with them, the same story over and over again. They built their perception of us based on our former master's rumors. How weird people are. They don't look for facts, don't see facts, or don't want to hear facts. Stereotypes and stigmas were like our shadows, and followed us everywhere we went. People hear rumors and believe them without trying to confirm their veracity. Unfortunately, this situation was an example of the swamp in which the spirit of our sport sank. We had tried to constructively impact these ingrained patterns with our positive attitude and respectful behavior, but without any results. Enduring prejudice like this was a curse that stuck with us.

World Cadet Championship August 4, 2019: Tashkent, Uzbekistan (Jonah)

If there are no obstacles to overcome, dreams are worthless. That was our motto at that time; the time when facing the rumors spread by our former master became part of our journey. His lies accompanied our names, and his decisive charge to destroy us was the sword that shattered our souls. No coach or master at that time had the courage to step in and try to represent the time-honored principles our sport was known to espouse. Black belts in martial arts represent self-discipline and morality, but these adults showed none.

The title of "Master" is honorary, a distinct title given to coaches who have mastered martial arts principles. But unfortunately, those coaches and masters who witnessed our torment and did nothing to stop our suffering do not have the right to hold that honorable and distinguished title. Therefore, we decided to train our minds to adapt to any situation we encountered. We decided to remain our own. No matter the circumstances, we needed to always be prepared.

We must embrace our dreams, persist in our uniqueness, and follow our path. Despite the stereotypes that had been following us and the stigmas that accompanied our names, we would not let these negative voices keep us away from our primary goal: controlling our state of mind. We went through a very long and arduous process of developing a growth mindset.

At the age of 10, Sally and me were forced to train in our garage — at that time we swore together to work hard and prepare to make it to the World Cadet Championships.

Sally and me at Uzbekistan airport — we were excited to be part of a world championship; we made it this far together

World Championship, Uzbekistan, 2019

World Championships, at the competition registration for our credentials, Uzbekistan, 2019

Jonah at the ring; During The World Championship, he was born again and found his purpose in life

We couldn't change people's stereotypes of us, but we could ignite our passion and desire for success by using these negative forces as motivation to inspire our passion to triumph over our minds. The only way to achieve our goals was to fly above the negativity. We knew it was better to stay true to who we were, even if the price was being alone. We would never give up, even if no one was willing to stand by us—even if the *world* stood against us, we would keep fighting. The best part of our journey was that Sally and I shared it. In unity, there is strength.

Sports and education played crucial roles in shaping our personalities and enriching our skills. They complement each other; education opened our minds to new possibilities and illuminated our minds with new ideas. As a result, we became more passionate about our goals and dreams and started to see a world outside of our sport. We began thinking in different directions about how to use our sport to achieve success. But, regardless of what kind of achievement we realized, we needed to use the sound principles of our sport; and draw the positive face of our sport away from the dark, the bullies, the abuse, and the negative forces. We had to show our former master, and the many other coaches who followed him, that the beauty of our sport lies in its principles; principles it is incumbent upon us to magnify within ourselves. We needed to nurture the ancient spirit of our sport. Currently, our sport appeared to focus on politics, medals, podiums, money, racism, and communication. The spirit of sport in Taekwondo waned long ago, but we could bring it to life again by adopting the principles and the discipline of our sport and adapting them to every aspect of our life.

Passion is the master of all success, and we will not stop until we can embrace ourselves and triumph over our minds. This is our hardest battle, but we must win it. It is all up to us now. We just need to believe in our abilities. Then, when we have a goal and we comprehend our purpose, we will have a clear vision and nothing will stop us.

After a long period of continuous training in the home garage, we began to show a very drastic change in our performance and attitude. Our professionalism in the sport and our constructive leadership became noticeable to all. We earned our qualifications for the World Cadet Championship. We continued to educate ourselves, enrich our minds, and develop strategies that helped us survive our battle. We finally began to see the light at the end of the tunnel.

Our preparation for the World Cadet Championship began on the first day we were forced to train in our garage. Bullies unknowingly gave us the positive motivation we needed to continue our battle to find our identity, the fight for our dream, and to free our minds. We had starved the distractions and fueled our focus during the years we were isolated in the garage. We concentrated on our academic excellence and the journey developing our mental strength.

Consequently, being isolated in the garage increased our chances of success. While many believed that if they bullied us, abused us, and separated us in our garage it would hurt us, our isolation was the perfect environment to work on developing the power of our minds, redirecting our thoughts, energy, and emotions onto an intensely positive path. Five years training in the garage made our way of thinking sharper and more practical. In every obstacle we encountered we saw a challenge that we had to overcome.

The daily words of encouragement and motivational speeches from our mother fueled our souls. Our mother was our life coach. She was able to counteract all the negative influences inflicted upon us by our bullies, as well as, our former master, and his abusive behaviors. Our mother was wise. She worked toward feeding our minds with positive conversations during the day and encouraging our spirit every night.

We were developing in a way that was different from athletes our age. Our maturity level increased rapidly, and our academic performance exceeded that of our peers. We started to perform very impressively in school and earned the respect of teachers and principals. The shift in our attitudes and personalities distinguished us from our peers, and bullies started noticing us. We were working on developing ourselves and focusing on our purpose by blocking out the distractions and negative voices that were meant to break us, while learning to forgive our abusers so that we could heal and be successful. We were preparing for the World Cadet Championships from a small garage, but publicly displaying the hearts of lions.

The World Cadet Championship was not an ordinary tournament for us: it was our celebration of victory. We traveled to Uzbekistan with a fierce mindset, determined to succeed not by standing on the podium or wearing a medal, but by showing everyone who stood in our way that we don't break. Making it to the World Championships was our first official step toward building a strong foundation for a great future for both of us, not only in sports, but life as a general.

We arrived in Uzbekistan a week before the competition so that we could train and adapt to the new environment. We were grouped with the U.S. National team, taking the same bus and staying at the same hotel. It was as if God wanted to send a message. The coaches who rejected and tried to break us were now witnessing our success. We trained alone and on our own time. How amazing it was to see ourselves standing among the best athletes in the world having come from our tiny garage.

August 9, 2019, was the day of my [Jonah's] fight. The Olympic coach had only arrived in town the night before and we hadn't even seen him yet as he was busy with his friends and the other coaches. I was utterly convinced of my abilities and was determined to be completely satisfied with the result of the match, regardless of what it was.

That day, I was there for myself, to declare my own identity. I had my first fight and felt like I owned the place. I was very comfortable and enjoyed the match. For the first time, I didn't even notice the Olympic coach. I felt like no one was sitting in my chair because I didn't need anyone in that chair. I was self-assured and won my first fight. The Olympic coach wasn't focused on me, but that didn't matter. I was completely confident, both emotionally and mentally.

In my quarter-final match, which would allow me to win a medal, I faced a powerful, taller opponent, who seemed more mature. I stood firmly against him and fought without surrendering. He would kick me and throw me to the ground, however, the more he attacked, the more I determined became to stand up and continue the fight. At that moment, I felt a change within myself. I knew my mindset had evolved. I finished my battle with honor, proud that I did not let the obstacles I encountered in the ring make me stop fighting, or give up. I never let the Olympic coach's recklessness and ignorance impact my mind and affect my performance. Even though I ultimately lost that day, I won a much more valuable and priceless battle: I won back myself. I had scored a victory in the fight against fear, doubt, indecision, weakness, low self-esteem, and, most importantly, our former master.

On that day, I was born again and found my purpose in life. I cried both because I had not earned a medal, but also because I had triumphed over those bullies. Sport is not a profession, a job, or a goal to be achieved. Sport is a way in which we adapt to reach our purpose in life and acquire skills to help us healthily live our lives.

I could just hear my parents cheering loudly for me and congratulating me on overcoming my obstacles. Sally ran toward me, hugged me tight, and jumped happily to tell me that I looked different in the ring, that I was strong, determined to win, and unbreakable. I looked around to see the Olympic coach but couldn't find him. He had already left to catch up with his friends.

On our way out of the convention center, we saw the coach from afar, talking and laughing with a group of fellow coaches. I felt really proud of myself at that moment; proud because these kinds of bullying behaviors didn't bother me anymore. These negative forces would no longer find their way into my mind and heart. I turned my back, looked at the Olympic coach, and felt sorry for him. I felt sorry that he missed the last chance I gave him to earn my respect. Sally was more disappointed with the Olympic coach's attitude than I was. She had hoped in her heart that he would change his attitude toward us, especially after he began to visit us with his family. Sadly, this was not the case.

The next day was Sally's fight day. Sally had her own way of manipulating her opponent and winning her matches. As Sally confidently walked toward the ring, we all waved to her from where we were seated. We were encouraging and showed our support to her. Sally and the Olympic coach both took their places in the ring, waiting for the referee to call the start of the match. While they waited, the coach leaned toward Sally and spoke to her. Sally's face turned pale white within seconds, as if she had seen a ghost. We were still cheering and waving to her, but she seemed to be in a different world and ignored us.

After the referee started the match, Sally took her first step into the ring. She looked different and wasn't herself. The match started, and I could tell Sally's mind wasn't focused on the fight. It was strange to see Sally act recklessly about her fight, a match she had been dreaming of and planning for many years. Sally was dodging her opponent's kicks. She was holding back, trying not to get involved with her opponent. Sally was avoiding a fight and didn't raise her leg to kick at all.

The match ended with a tough loss for Sally. We were all in shock as this was the first time we saw Sally incapacitated like this. The coach left Sally after she finished her fight, and we didn't see him after the match. Sally walked her way to the conference center door with heavy steps, keeping her head down in an attempt to hide her pain. We knew immediately that Sally needed to leave, so we hugged her and got her out of there. We gave her space to freshen up and didn't put any pressure on her to talk.

When she was ready, Sally raised her face to look at our dad, and in a moment, mixed with ignorance, despair, and strength, she said, "It doesn't matter anymore; he's like the others." She went on to say that the Olympic coach had whispered in her ear "She is stronger than you" right before her fight. It was the only thing he said to her, but it was enough to completely shake her confidence. Sally was shocked to hear those words from the person who was supposed to be sitting in her chair to motivate and support her. Because of the Olympic coach, Sally became distracted and demoralized. She gave up and couldn't fight that day. Sally lost her battle and lost her trust in others. Sally refused to fight that day as she had blocked out her abilities. She chose to lose—not because she wanted to—but because at that moment she had lost all hope. She saw our sport as a delusion and refused to participate in this delusion.

We couldn't sleep that night and were supremely disappointed with the Olympic coach. How could he be so cruel? How could he betray us in this way? How dare he be so ruthless toward us?

Early the next morning we took the bus and headed to the airport. We left Uzbekistan with honor and many lessons learned. The day we left was the last time we saw the Olympic coach. He had shown us his true colors when he decided to destroy us right before sending us into battle on the world stage. Our chapter with him had finally come to an end.

Sadly, we later found out that the Olympic coach did what he did because we had stopped paying him his monthly fee. The fee that we had been paying him for over a year for a service we never received. The fee that we gave him to help him and his partner dig themselves out of a financial hole. The fee over which his new partner had finally decided wasn't worth angering our former master.

Despite all this, we accepted the truth and went back to training in our garage. We were determined to heal ourselves and remain positive. We continued to pursue our vision, convinced that a new chapter was opening up for us, one free of pain and disrespect. Our scars were not fully healed, but the pain was finally ebbing.

Once again, we decided to concentrate only on the positive. We had both qualified for the World Cadet Championships and participated in the World Championships. We had demonstrated that sport is not a political stage on which to manifest false discourse about athletes' rights, goals, and dreams. Sport is an opportunity given to everyone who has a dream inside of them, together with those who are ready to succeed and achieve this dream—regardless of race, religion, or gender. Sport is for everyone, and every person has the right to participate. No one, whatever their authority, has the right to disregard the law, violate humanitarian rules, or dismiss the rights of children to live their dreams and practice their sport in a peaceful environment free from abuse, threat, terror, and discrimination. Sports provides an educational vehicle for acquiring life skills, and no one has the right to block anyone's path to accessing and benefitting from these educational opportunities.

We look back now and see how young we were—our childhoods were forcibly stolen from us by the repetitive and hurtful battles we had to face to overcome our pain. We matured quickly, and although we lost our early childhood, we earned respect and forged our identities. We had demonstrated that children are capable of far more than others give them credit for. Children have power, and their voices should be heard. Children can have a vision; they can set goals and they can have dreams. Children can thrive, work hard, and conquer. We all have strengths inside of us, but we need to empower those forces. We must have confidence in ourselves, believe in our abilities, and be patient.

We ended up graduating from middle school with the Presidential Academic Excellence Award and the National Honor Society Distinguished Achievement Award, an outstanding award based on our participation in community service, best citizenship, leadership, and excellent scholarship. We received the President's Gold Award for Community Service. We were awarded the Congressional Award for Setting and Accomplishing Important Goals. Most importantly, we created a non-profit organization, *"The Power Within,"* to help children who face struggles, obstacles, and limitations that prevent them from achieving their goals. We all have powers within us, but we need the right vision to find them. We have the power to give, share, help, conquer, accomplish, heal, learn, educate, empower, and dream. And now we have this book, *The Night Blooming: A Journey of Teen Twin Champions Overcoming Racism, Rejection & Abuse, To Find Their Identity & Purpose In Life*, that we know will help children find their own purpose in life just as we did.

CHAPTER TWELVE
The Power Within (Jonah)

"Find your passion, develop your vision, arm yourself with discipline, and focus on your goal. Hold on to your dreams, unchain your powers, and own your story. Never stop dreaming. Giving up is not an option."

These were our mother's daily motivational words to us—since the first day of Spring 2017, the official day we were forced into isolation, training in our garage. We understood the heavy weight we were compelled to carry on our shoulders. On one hand, we carried the responsibilities and obligations toward our education. On the other hand, we had to bear the weight of even more responsibility toward our mission, our goal, and our dream. Do we allow our former master to win, stealing our dreams with his abusive and decisive actions, or do we empower ourselves, redirecting our focus toward strengthening our minds? This question has led to a long journey toward developing a growth mindset for both of us.

We chose a rigorous path that took many years out of our childhood and forced us to mature too fast. We found that a positive attitude is an essential component of developing a strong mindset in difficult times. It is this positive attitude that helped us overcome the difficulties, limitations, and obstacles we encountered during our isolation. It made it easier for us to develop our abilities in a very conservative way which led us to our success.

One's mentality is the mental strength of both mind and body—the ability to overcome challenges or the way obstacles are perceived. Our mother repeatedly reminded us that our mental strength would prevail in the darkest times and the most challenging days. She also told us never to let any uncertain circumstance weaken our minds. Mom equipped us to work on strengthening our minds as this was the only key to our success later in life. It is this mindset that set us apart from everyone else in our sport and school. It's not that we are smarter than our peers or stronger than our fellow athletes, it's just that we are able to focus our minds and approach difficult situations with a positive attitude. We chose to never encounter a challenge with fear but, rather, with confidence and smiles on our faces.

Sally and me at the garage during one of our sparring sessions together

Sally covers her eyes during a training session to embrace our mental and sensory abilities

Sally is in our backyard during a sweltering summer after we finished a tough physical training session

Sally is on one of our tough summer workouts in our backyard working on resistance and strength

Sally and I during one of our cycling sessions to increase our speed and leg strength

We both show courtesy and respect for each other before we start sparring together

Sally and I after our training, singing and expressing our joy — The garage training became our shelter

Sally and I working on our footwork drills, at the garage

Sally and I at the garage, during one of our sparring sessions together

Sally and I at the garage empowering kids around the world and sending positive vibes to them

Me (Jonah) during my garage training working on empowering my kicks

Sally and I preparing for our sparring session together

Since we were young, we have been the victims of mental and emotional harassment at the hands of bullies, peers, and even coaches. We were constantly called names and laughed at, both at school and in Taekwondo. These were dark times. However, after a while, we realized that these people were just background noise and the only way to keep them quiet was through our success. Our Taekwondo instructors left us with no choice but to train in our home garage. Ironically, training in our garage ended up giving us a new perspective on life. Training alone in that small space showed us that we could achieve anything we put our minds to—and that no matter how many walls were put up in front of us, we would never give up, because we knew there were great things for us lie ahead.

Sally and Me in our garage — After more than five years of training in our garage, we successfully conquered all of our fears. We could not have done so without belief in the power within ourselves, so we decided to create a non-profit organization: ***The Power Within***

Sally at the track field of the neighborhood high school during winter time training

Sally and I at the track field training together, working on our flexibility

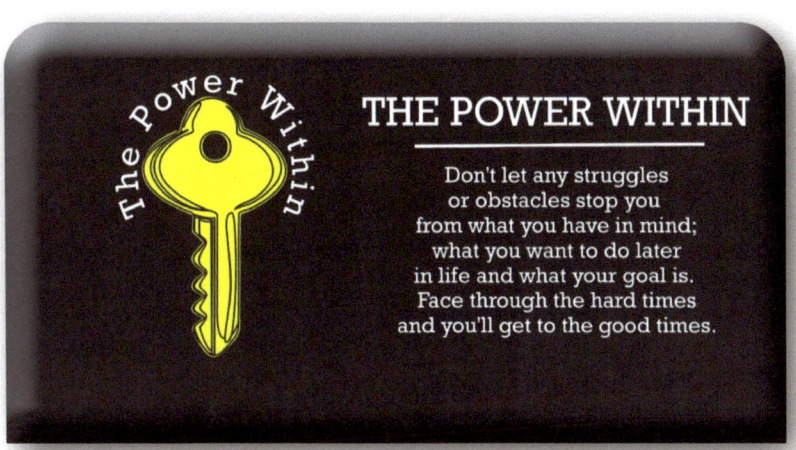

Card with our non-profit organization's motto. Our main goal is to spread positivity. Our mission is to inspire and help young members of our community—regardless of gender, background, race, religion, and color—to reach their goals and fulfill their dreams, just as we did. We desire to make a positive impact by empowering education and instilling a love of knowledge

Sally and I after we finished our running session during the winter

Sally in the garage working on her leg flexibility

Sally and I after our poem the Power Within Won the Contest of Poetry Grand slam

Success and a strong mindset don't care if a person is strong, weak, old, young, girl, boy, black, white, rich or poor, Muslim, Christian, or Jewish. Success and a strong mindset come from a willingness to be different from others. If we are smart about the choices we make in life; if we keep moving forward no matter what lies ahead; and if we have a positive attitude through the challenges and difficulties of our lives. Finally, if we have confidence in ourselves and brush aside the negative things someone says or does to us, it is our positive mindset that will get us through challenging and difficult times in our lives. Our constructive mindset will always be there for us when we go down a dark path. Our strong mindset will be the light in the darkness; it will be the thing that keeps us going until we reach the end of our path. Our confident mindset is the attribute that helps us deal with life's curve balls; it is the thing that empowers our abilities, our hopes, and our dreams.

Pain, Prosperity, and Strength (2021)

A confined place with limited space in which to move ended up allowing us to be challenged to figure out how we could overcome our limitations and discover our purpose. Through more than five years of rejection and isolation, we realized that the best race to run is the race against yourself and your limits. Earning medals was a physical goal that was necessary to prove to our former master that he could not stop us from achieving success. Fulfilling our dreams, continuing to be ourselves, and following our paths were the important goals.

We faced many challenges and struggles, but despite these difficulties, we still maintained our positive attitudes and focused closely on our goals. Our unique mental strengths facilitated our phenomenal academic achievements. We mastered our first year of high school with full remote learning, during a full year of quarantine in our home. We experienced a very peaceful and healthy journey through remote learning, as those years of training alone in our garage had taught us to stay strong mentally and not give into depression, fear, or despair.

After more than five years of training in our garage, we had successfully conquered all of our fears. We could not have done so without belief in the power within ourselves. Our main goal in creating *The Power Within* is to spread positivity. Our core mission is to inspire and aid young members of our community—regardless of gender, background, race, religion, and color—reach their goals and fulfill their dreams, just as we did. We seek to make a positive impact by empowering others to study, instilling a love of reading, and encouraging the acquisition of knowledge. In other words, we deeply desire to use the lessons we learned during our struggles to help others.

Our Takeaways

We have always believed that it is through positive behavior that change can occur. Children are the future, and if we work together to improve each other's lives our world will be a better place. We both have been through many difficult experiences, which have made us realize that we all need each other to grow. We can fulfill our dreams at the same time we pave the way for others to succeed—as seeing others happy, makes us happy.

Motivation: We can motivate ourselves and others—especially young children—to have confidence in their abilities and to believe in themselves. The belief we had in ourselves and our abilities helped motivate us to keep going even when we felt all alone. Many times, we had to give ourselves encouraging pep talks to carry on. We had to push away the negativity so that we wouldn't get lost in despair.

Confidence: Over the last few difficult years, and despite everything we'd been through, we remained confident in ourselves—which is reflected in every situation we encountered. This confidence, enabled us to view challenging situations rationally. Being confident, knowing that we had developed skilled coping techniques, gave us the ability to understand the consequences of our actions, and the courage to face those consequences.

Problem-solving skills: Through our many trials and challenges we developed far-reaching problem-solving skills. We learned to respond quickly and professionally to issues we encounter, as well as, find valuable and immediate solutions to our problems. The Covid-19 Pandemic, which began in March 2020, was challenging for all of us—especially students. Distance learning was difficult and required students to adapt and learn new skills. We found ourselves applying some of the same problem-solving techniques we developed training alone in our garage, to the issues we faced on account of quarantine. Maintaining a healthy mindset through it all was key.

Leadership skills: We have led ourselves to achieve our ultimate goals, despite very challenging circumstances. This experience has enhanced our leadership skills and gave us the right tools to help others—by guiding them positively toward achieving their dreams and goals.

Developing vision: Our five years of training in our garage empowered us to fully develop our vision for our future. Our vision was lofty, but realistic. We saw what we wanted to do and how we could accomplish it. We were disciplined and organized in achieving that vision. We feel confident that we can help others develop their visions for their future.

Strong mindset: We are very determined athletes, students, and human beings. This determination helped us achieve our goals and defeat our challenges, and through this quality, we were able to reach out to children and other athletes and help them work toward their goals and dreams, impacting them positively and providing techniques that can help strengthen their mind sets.

Open-minded: We had to train for over five years in the garage because our former master and his fellow coaches punished us for something we didn't do—and because we called them out to "Stop bullying and abusing us." The behaviors of our former master and other coaches made us realize that respect is based on people's willingness to be open-minded toward one another, and ready to receive criticism, or listen to a different opinion.

We grew up in a family with different values, norms, and cultural beliefs than those of our neighbors and peers. This unique experience allowed us to understand that there are differences between people. We opened our minds to accepting these differences, finding the right way to adapt, as well as discovering a variety of positive solutions and ways to interact with others. We were taught to respect everyone, even if their beliefs differed from our own.

Positive attitude: Maintaining a positive attitude has made all the difference in our lives. With all that we've been through it would have been easy to let the negativity seep in but we remained determined to find the right path to overcoming our difficulties. As a result, we have become goal-driven people, who have helped many children— both older and younger than us—direct their focus on setting goals and working toward those goals rather than concentrating on the problem itself.

Values: Deep-rooted values have been our faithful friends in difficult times. Experience taught us that discipline, morals, and principles can radically change the lives of young people and children. Through these fundamental ethical guidelines, young men and women can teach themselves to distinguish right from wrong. Moreover, values can build a strong foundation for future leaders in our society. Values are powerful ingredients for nurturing a healthy generation, able to replace negative emotions with positive ones, by virtue of their ability to discern what is right and what is wrong. We believe that our positive attitude and the values we uphold have played an essential role in maintaining the consistency of our beliefs; helping us enhance our respect for others; forging our ability to experience empathy, show compassion, and empowering the humanity within ourselves.

Resilience: Through the many challenges we faced, we developed a mindset of resilience and determination to keep moving forward. Setbacks served as motivational catalyst that helped reinforce our determination and passion for being better than we were before.

Taking full responsibility: We are very responsible young people, who accept responsibility for setting goals, accomplishing tasks, and completing jobs. We have developed this quality through facing challenges, while still taking full responsibility for striving toward our dreams, remaining focused on our mission to achieve each of our goals.

Finding our purpose: During our journey in the garage, our focus slowly shifted from "just" Taekwondo training, toward preparing for the primary purpose of our lives: to help, empower, and support other children emotionally and mentally through their own life journeys.

Our future research and career: Our journey into the unknown eased our passion for studying the mind, our mysterious friend during our quest toward inner strength and self-assurance. We developed a growth mindset through more than five years of challenges that helped nourish our minds. We traveled with our minds on a journey that reinforced the importance of the human psyche in developing resilience and identifying optimal solutions to the many challenges we faced. This journey made us more passionate about studying and researching the human mind and focusing on our future careers in the field of neuroscience. We became curious to study how our brains transition from a fragile mindset, to a strong and resilient mindset, and then eventually, reach a growth mindset.

All the medals we earned during training at our garage—Taekwondo Achievements

Reflection (Sally and Jonah)

Our childhood was not ordinary. It was full of disappointments and challenges to our abilities. Nevertheless, our childhood experiences made us into the people we are today. It shaped our perception of life and ourselves.

We were born into a very traditional family with two loving parents. Our family was different from other families around us, as our parents were immigrants who had come to the United States hoping to fulfill their dreams, and find a better lifestyle in which to start a family. This difference made us the targets of bullies in school, and later in Taekwondo. However, our mother always nourished and nurtured our minds with positivity and guided us through many of the tough times we faced. We watched her, searching daily for ways to help us overcome our many challenges and obstacles. From her, we learned how to be independent and loyal and how to have a vision. We learned how to build a bridge between our hearts and God and how to have deep faith in Him. Our mother is our hero and role model, and we have been watching her trying to overcome her own obstacles, and facing her own battles over the years. We have learned how to be responsible for our future because we have seen how responsible she was for ensuring a very successful future for us. She taught us how to be independent by amplifying the importance of education in our lives.

Through education, we found our identities. Through her bold dignity, we learned how to be proud of ourselves and how to value ourselves. Our mother taught us how to be determined in our achieving goals, because she is determined to help us reach our goals.

She showed us how to have a spiritual relationship with God and how to trust Him concerning our destiny. Through her love of God, she showed us a strong, inner peace. She showed us by example how if we trust God in our destiny, we will be at peace with ourselves.

She taught us how we can have a vision—a vision for ourselves, our dreams, our goals, and our family. It opened our eyes to seeing many opportunities and having the strength and the will to embark on these opportunities. Our mom taught us how to be true to our vision, work hard and elevate our abilities to make that dream come true. Our mother encouraged us to see the obstacles we encountered as new opportunities to grow, thrive, and continue to strive for more. She has provided us with the privilege to live in an optimistic world through her positive attitude, motivational words, behaviors, and actions.

After several years of fighting against negativity and listening to our mother's optimistic voice, we can now look at ourselves and realize that we've achieved our goals. We have both developed strong characters. We have cast off fear and live a principled life. Today, after more than seven years of painful isolation training in our garage, we want our mother to know that she is still our hero and role model— and that without her we would not be the people we are today. We want to thank her for teaching us the true meaning of being a leader; showing us by example how to lead. We followed in her footsteps and were able to guide ourselves to find our inner strength and our life's purpose. As a result, we have shaped our own identities of which we are very proud.

Colors

Black and white are opposite colors, both reflecting bold messages. Black represents strength, darkness, death, ignorance, loss, and fear; while white represents purity, light, perfection, a new beginning, freshness, and, most importantly, positivity. Colors are an essential descriptive element in our lives. Colors can represent our identities and our personalities. In life, we go experience many events and these events carry different colors within them. Sometimes, we tend to get lost in the dark colors by the uncertain decisions and choices we make. We may add bright colors, or dark colors to our experiences— but we have choices to make, and through these choices, we paint our lives with the colors that reflect who we are.

During the many years of solitary training in our garage, we wisely chose to add bright colors to our journey—even though it was filled with uncertainty, we forced our minds to see the positive in every obstacle we encountered. Our garage used to be just a room with white walls. However, once we learned to fully embrace the challenges that we encountered, we decided to paint those walls a bright, positive color, representative of our new and improved attitudes.

We believe that not every setback is a failure, and sometimes—in exceptional situations—setbacks clearly indicate the beginning of prosperity and growth. Skeptics, haters, and externalities ruled our lives, belittling our ability to have control over ourselves and crippling our creativity. But, we learned to thrive in the darkness of our garage, just as the night-blooming cactus does. The night-blooming cactus is a type of cactus that blooms only at night and has a very bright white color with a strong aroma. For us, this bright white flower represents our story of defeating the darkness around us, while reclaiming the hope in our dreams and the passion within our hearts.

Over the many years that we had trained alone in our garage, so far, we had few opportunities for social interactions with coaches, athletes, or our peers at school. We had no choice but to train our minds to persist against obstacles, difficulties, and adversity. With our passion and strong will to continue to fight to achieve our goals, we grew up and learned, survived, and conquered. Through perseverance, we learned how to be strong. Being isolated in the garage allowed us to reveal our inner strength, fly high, and return to our nest with a passion to thrive. We learned through years of painful training alone in our garage that we have the strength within us to choose to be optimistic and to focus on the positive things in our lives. We forced ourselves to draw out the optimism within us, even when darkness covered every aspect of our lives. Optimism added valuable meaning to our journey, and was the spirit that gave us a reason to push ourselves to continue the journey we started together. We have seen within our limits a new level of possibility to discover a vision within us, the strength to reach new levels of training, and the boundless courage to live our dreams, while conscious of the intense darkness surrounding us.

We needed to conquer our attitudes, master our mental capabilities, and reach our full mindset growth. We shattered our limits and our flows of progress surged. Optimism changed our perception of everything we encounter and will continue to positively impact everything we face later in life.

Sally and I are in our garage, where we set up our non-profit "The Power Within,"—where we've been training for a cause, the funding of backpacks and school supplies for underprivileged children

Sally and me

Sally and me helping needy children and promoting the importance of education by funding education-related projects

Our non-profit project, "Training for a Cause"—for three years we raised funding for backpacks and school supplies for underprivileged children

Sally and I listen to a mother who needs school supplies for her primary school during a community backpacks for kids campaign

Jonah and I at Children's Health Medical Center, where we funded 100 backpacks full of school supplies for sick kids

Sally and I are on our way to our first day of high school

Sally and I through one of our campaigns empowering girls around the world

Jonah and I are in the garage filling backpacks with school supplies to give to disadvantaged children in our community.

Jonah and I are full of positivity working in our garage on filling backpacks with school supplies for underrepresented children

Sally and I are at our McMillen High School where Sally and I awarded The Pride of McMillen and the highest recognition awards

Jonah and I work on our non-profit organizations project to eliminate literacy and empower education within underprivileged communities in Africa

Sally and I with Academic awards

Sally and I during one of PAL- Peer Leadership Assistance training sessions

Sally and I got inducted in the National Spanish Honor Society

Jonah and I have been awarded the National Junior Honor Society Outstanding Achievement Award

Jonah and I filling backpacks with school supplies

Jonah and I with the Congress Recognition Award for setting and achieving important goals

Sally and I on our way to deliver backpacks to underprivileged children in our community

Our Poem "Dear Pain" won first place the Grand Slam of McMillen

Jonah and I were nominated to participate in The Congress of Future Medical conference by Nobel Prize in Medicine Dr. Mario Cappecchi

Sally and I are in our garage working on a project to promote education and raise awareness of the importance of education

Jonah and I are at our McMillen High School

Jonah during a meditation session

Sally and I are in our Dobok, Taekwondo uniform,
on our way to empowering underprivileged kids

Jonah and I working on enabling literacy, and empowering kids through reading at our garage

We are at our garage working toward our goal of enabling literacy, empowering a love of reading among underprivileged children all over the world

Sally and I are in our garage, as we begin our campaign to enable worldwide literacy among children in need

Sally is at our high school where she was awarded our School Pride Award, Mr. Todd Williams, our high school principal presents her with the Award

Jonah is at our high school where he was awarded the highest esteem distinction award by the National Honor Society for most volunteers hours of community service and community support. Award presented by Mr. Todd Williams, our McMillen High School principal

Authors' Quotes

▲ Life doesn't come with a road map or instructions; we must travel through life alone, trying to reach our chosen destinations. What ultimately makes someone strong is how they react to the twists and turns that life throws at them.

▲ The pain we feel today is the basis for our success tomorrow; injustice, abuse, rejection and bullying are harsh, but the seeds of determination that grow within us for success are stronger than any hardships.

▲ When you have a firm belief in yourself, adversity cannot shake your heart.

▲ Don't let any struggles or obstacles stop you from what you have in mind, what you want to do later in life, and what your goal is. Face the hard times, and you will get to the good times.

▲ We have to embrace the struggles, challenge ourselves, and study our capabilities further.

▲ To become stronger, we must focus more deeply on what is most important.

▲ The moment you overcome the things that were trying to limit your capabilities, you will realize that you are on the right path to developing unlimited growth for your mind and body.

▲ To grow mentally, you have to face your limitations and defeat your obstacles.

▲ Build a bridge between your heart and mind, and gain wings to help you overcome your obstacles by flying above your limits.

▲ Pain can clear our minds and allow us to discover the vital force that lives within us.

▲ Repetition is a vital learning method in training. Repeating the same exercise over and over will help store our skills in our subconscious mind, making training easier over time.

▲ A dream is never just a dream, it is a goal with high expectations and continuous hard work.

▲ We may feel like our feet are tied to obstacles and we can't move to change our destiny, but with every hit we take, we have the choice to fight back and try to keep our balance. We can try to fight back.

▲ Because we have such a strong belief in our purpose, we never give up on overcoming the obstacles we encounter.

▲ Our purpose is stronger than the obstacles that try to limit our strength. Garage training is the story of our struggles and defeats. We defeated the four walls that were trying to suffocate our souls.

▲ When you have the power to control the things that limit you, you are on the right track to developing unlimited growth for your mind and body.

▲ In a broken heart lives a strong will to rise again.

▲ In any unpleasant situation, there is growth.

▲ Be the champion you always look up to. Be the catalyst for your success. Be the person you want to be. Be yourself.

▲ When you know your destination, you walk with confidence.

▲ We come to a path with two ends, we pause and hesitate as to which one to adopt, but in the end we follow our courage in the hope that there is a bright future at the end of this path.

▲ Your inner strength is the most powerful motivational force you can have. Believe in yourself.

▲ We face darkness and limitations during our journey, but what keeps us excited about our journey is our belief that we can overcome our limitations and make ourselves better than we were yesterday.

▲ The path you take alone has the most powerful results. You are capable of more than you know.

▲ True motivation is driven by a strong purpose.

▲ Controlling the things that were trying to limit our capabilities was the first indication that we were on the right track to develop unlimited growth for our mind and body. Garage training for years was the most painful and most important experience we had as children, however, we were stronger than our adversity, and we defeated the abusers and bullies with our passion for the sport we love and our resilience to continue the journey despite the pain that has been burning in our hearts for years.

▲ We all have a winner inside us, but not all of us have the right mindset to awaken the winner within; We have to believe in ourselves, commit to action and push ourselves to the edge as the winner within us emerges.

▲ Never underestimate the power of your mind.

▲ The greatest champion is the one who constantly competes with himself.

▲ When you feel you can't give more, remember how you started and how far you've come.

▲ Failure is necessary to kindle the fire within us and embrace our passion to move forward to try again and again; rising after failure is victory.

▲ If you have a small belief in your abilities deep in your heart, keep at it, and never stop trying because that small belief will grow with you and become your purpose in life.

▲ We may start small, but how far we can go depends on our passion and desire to grow exponentially.

▲ Discipline is the only weapon with which we arm ourselves to enable our minds to understand how capable we are, even when huge obstacles and limitations surround us.

▲ In dark times, strength is born.

▲ Be fierce in the face of adversity, be bold, have faith in your abilities, and believe that you can weather any storm that comes your way.

▲ No matter how many times you have felt defeated by obstacles, challenges, rejection, or stuck in a hopeless situation, remind yourself that you are stronger than any barriers you face because you have strength and power within you.

▲ The greatest and most valuable victory is one achieved in the dark, where there is no crowd applauding you, no one acknowledging your talent, no platform to stand on. It is a victory over your minds, your doubts, your fears, and the obstacles that stand in your way.

▲ No matter what stands in your way, you must believe that you have the strength within you to overcome any limitations, obstacles, and challenges to achieve your success and reach your goal.

▲ Speed is a skill that plays an important role in enabling our brain to think and act quickly to send many commands to the muscles of the body in response to movement and reaction training.

▲ Without a deep belief in your abilities, you cannot overcome your fear of stepping out of your comfort zone.

▲ Your muscles are flexible, and they can resume their normal shape after being stretched, and your brain has the ability to control your muscles to stretch as much as you want them to. So trust your own mind.

▲ We keep training hard, learning, developing and dreaming because with our commitment to making our dreams come true, we can go far.

▲ Keep growing, and don't stop until you become the person you want to be.

▲ It only takes one shot to take your abilities to the next level.

▲ When you reach the final destination and look back, you will see that the many hours of hard work and the amount of effort you put in was because of your strong belief in your abilities and determination to succeed. You will realize that your success is unique because it was achieved by your own knowledge and abilities.

▲ Being aware of your physical and mental capabilities is vital to your success.

▲ Perfection never comes easy; it is a long journey of continuous hard work.

▲ Hard work is not an option, but it is a must if we want to succeed.

▲ The only battle you want to win is the battle against your own fear and self-doubt.

▲ Live with passion.

▲ Keep your soul alive.

▲ We must never stop trying until we can fully embrace ourselves and conquer the fears inside our minds. This is our hardest battle.

▲ We strive to conquer. But, to keep moving forward, we must have a passion and desire to create a meaningful life. We have to live a relentless life and kindle the passion within us. We have to prevail over our limitations and make our own way.

▲ In any uncomfortable situation you encounter, there is potential for growth. See your difficulties as an opportunity for growth.

▲ We strive to train not to find ourselves, but to create ourselves.

▲ The power is ours. The journey is ours. The gift is ours. We are the only ones upon whom we can rely. We are the only ones who control our success.

▲ Train your brain to view obstacles as opportunities. Don't be afraid of the restrictions around you.

▲ To develop a strong mindset, we realized that we had to continue to resist obstacles and limitations. We had to challenge our minds to resist the force against us and empower the force within.

▲ We've learned that when everything around us turns black, we need to keep our hearts white, our minds bright, and our eyes shining with hope.

▲ The tough challenges we go through in our lives shape our thoughts and behaviors and try to force us to give up what we believe in, but the choice is in our hands to give up and never compromise.

▲ When confidence is found, we can overcome great obstacles and turn our toughest challenges into opportunities for our strongest defeats.

▲ Trust breeds unity, and unity leads to prosperity.

▲ Our thoughts are very powerful, and we must control what happens inside our minds. Through balance, we can focus, but we must choose what we focus on.

▲ We learned that our brain is a multi-functional system that can think, plan, manage, and give orders to our nerves and muscles. Our brain is the main operating system responsible for raising the level and intensity of our training by providing us with visual endurance, speed, reaction, and cognitive abilities.

▲ Mastering our attention required strong willpower. Strong willpower allowed us to intentionally ignore distractions, while staying focused on the task at hand.

▲ We have the power within us to create, dream, accomplish, heal, thrive, inspire, and overcome our limitations and obstacles.

▲ We can achieve our goals and dreams with deep faith and a strong will. Believe in your abilities and believe in yourself even if everyone doubts you. Even if you see darkness covering you. You are the only one who knows the power within your heart and mind. Only you know how to bring light into darkness. So, stay positive and keep your passion for the things you love to do.

▲ Learning how to fight and survive your obstacles while being constrained to use your full physical energy and ability is the ultimate strength. You need to conquer your mental growth.

▲ Break your limits.

▲ Be the bright side of your struggle; positivity comes from within.

▲ Never underestimate the power within you. Unleash your power.

▲ Motivation is the only fuel that helps us achieve our goals. Unfortunately, we always look for external motivation to fuel our enthusiasm, always forgetting that we have a powerful source of motivation inside of us. However, we don't need to look outside to find our motivation and kindle our inner fire.

▲ We just need to transcend our limits and obstacles to achieve our goals. We must know that we have a strong internal impulse within us that keeps us moving.

▲ Curiosity leads to new paths, intensifies the power of self-learning, and can fuel the power within us to conquer, learn, and discover.

▲ Elevate your obstacles to the highest level.

▲ Seeing your limits as a new level of possibility and opportunity is the power of clear vision, the strength to reach new levels of training, and the courage to live your dreams while being aware of the darkness around you.

▲ Our stubbornness confirmed our desire to continue the journey, despite all the limitations we encountered. It was a positive trait for both of us, not a negative one.

▲ Look at life's obstacles from a positive perspective.

▲ You have the power within you to break through obstacles and conquer your fears.

▲ Don't let your limits define your strength; instead, let your strength crush your limits and unleash your strength.

▲ Train your brain to keep fighting the obstacles and move forward. Don't stop moving even if your obstacles become heavy and try to drag you down.

▲ Simplicity is the beauty of life. The more you simplify the obstacles, the easier your journey will be.

▲ When you reach the end of your comfort zone, you will realize that there is no way back. You have to push hard, keep spinning faster, kick away your obstacles, and smash your limits. Your speed will take you to another life in a flash, where the real journey begins and new opportunities arise. Keep spinning fast.

▲ Obstacles cause pain, control our minds and drain our emotions. They steal our dreams and spread darkness around us, but we can overcome our obstacles by making the journey unforgettable and trying to fill it with happy moments. So let the sun rise, let the darkness fade away, and we believe that within each of us there is a powerful force that makes us heal and smile again.

▲ Training in the garage limited our creativity and tried to steal our positivity and motivation, but we both knew we had to learn to achieve balance in the narrow, limited paths we walked along on our journey. We needed to know how to stay on the right track and not get caught up in the obstacles that burdened us. We needed to learn to control our obstacles by controlling our steps.

▲ We both know that if we wanted to become stronger and more powerful, we must suffer as that is how we can develop resilience. We realized that the pain and disappointments we faced that day gave us another perspective on our purpose.

▲ Without proper control over our motor skills, we would be unable to apply our strength and flexibility in desired ways. We developed our motor skills, increased our sense of self-movement, and learned more about body position.

▲ There is always a new beginning at every opportunity. We have seen the unlimited possibilities that we can create with new beginnings.

▲ Colors are an essential descriptive element in our lives. Colors can represent our identities and our personalities. In life, we experience many events, and these events carry different colors within them. Sometimes, we tend to get lost in the dark colors by the uncertain decisions and choices we make in our lives. We may add bright colors and dark colors to our lives, but we have choices to make, and through these choices, we color our lives with the colors that reflect who we are.

▲ There will always be obstacles, adversity, challenges, doubters, and setbacks along the way. We may struggle to face all these difficulties, but without suffering and pain, we will never become stronger and smarter than before. We have a power within us that keeps whispering, telling us to keep moving, to keep trying, to believe in our abilities, and to trust in the process.

▲ Through action and reaction we learn how to develop our skills. The beauty of victory over our struggle is that it reactivates the power within us. How we act and react to our obstacles determines how we defeat them. We must be quick, but we must control our attitude toward the obstacles we face.

▲ You have the power within you to choose to be an optimist, to focus on the positive things in your life. Optimism will add light to darkness so choose to foster optimism within you during the darkest times.

▲ There are two different types of accomplishments in life. The first is what comes from the strength within us due to our endless efforts.

The second is the achievement that comes thanks to the help of others who paved the way for us. Although both are called accomplishments, with time only the original achievements remain the real ones. Those that we achieved without the help or approval of others. Choose wisely which one you want to achieve.

▲ Obstacles are essential to mental development, and it is through these obstacles that we learn to push ourselves away from our comfort zone. More importantly, obstacles teach us skills that we cannot learn from other experiences in our lives: how to develop our faith; how to stay positive; how we see everything around us reflecting bright light even if it is dark; and how to be happy on the inside.

▲ Our journey taught us that the more we stretch our awareness and challenge our limitations, the more resilient we become. We realized that if we wanted to survive and thrive, we needed to be flexible with the struggles we encountered. We needed to find the strength within us to expand our capabilities, limits, and patience. We must be flexible and adapt.

▲ Use your limits as fuel to increase your speed towards your growth potential.

▲ Obstacles are essential to mental development, and it is through these obstacles that we learn to push ourselves away from our comfort zone.

▲ We told ourselves that we needed to dig deep within ourselves to find our potential, to discover the powerful world that lay within us. We must dig deep within ourselves to find our inner strength. We must use our potential, ability, and strength to achieve our goals and overcome our obstacles. We knew we had a powerful force within us, and we needed to empower it.

▲ Fight your weakness and empower your strength.

▲ You have the power to explore your capabilities, expand your journey, strengthen your mentality, and overcome the limitations that were trying to force you to give up. You have the power within you to open new doors. Never underestimate your power.

▲ You have the inner strength to reach new heights, overcome your limitations, and break down the walls that surround you. Embrace your life to the fullest.

Our Congressional Award Ceremony • February 2023

www.ingramcontent.com/pod-product-compliance
Lightning Source LLC
Chambersburg PA
CBHW042258280426
43661CB00097BA/1181